LOCAL AREA NETWORKING FOR THE SMALL LIBRARY

SECOND EDITION

A How-To-Do-It Manual

Norman Howden

***HOW-TO-DO-IT MANUALS
FOR LIBRARIANS***

NUMBER 67

NEAL-SCHUMAN PUBLISHERS, INC.
New York, London

Published by Neal-Schuman Publishers, Inc.
100 Varick Street
New York, NY 10013

Printed and bound in the United States of America.

Library of Congress Cataloging-in-Publication Data

Howden, Norman.
    Local area networking for the small library : a how-to-do-it manual /
Norman Howden.—2nd ed.
        p.   cm.—(How-to-it manuals for librarians ; no. 67)
    Includes bibliographical references and index.
    ISBN 1-55570-285-6
    1. Local area networks (Computer networks)   2. Small libraries—Data
processing.   I. Title.   II. Series: How-to-do-it manuals for libraries ; no.
67.
Z678.93.L63H68   1996
021.6'5—dc20   96-29331

To new generations of
library and information science
students
who are learning
the importance
of information logistics

CONTENTS

Figures   ix
Preface   xi

1 What is a LAN?   1

   Components   2
   LAN Operations   3
   Planning   7
   Implementation   9
   Additional Resources   10

2 Operating Systems   11

   Compatibility   12
   System Organization   14
   Security   15
   Standards   17
   System Features   18
   Sub-LANs   19
   Utilities   19
   Additional Resources   21

3   Hardware   23

   Server   23
   Disk Drives   24
   Workstations and LAN Interface Cards   25
   Printer Options   27
   Gateways and Bridges   29
   Uninterruptible Power Supply and Backup Systems   30
   Security   32
   Additional Resources   34

4   Wiring   35

   Topology   35
   Survey   36
   Design and Layout   37
   Purchasing   38
   Installation   39
   Additional Resources   40

5   Applications   **43**

   Licensing   43
   Selection   44
   Library Systems   46
   Training   49
   Additional Resources   50

6 Start Up   **51**

   Site Planning   51
   Installation   53
   Additional Resources   60

7 Daily Operations   **61**

   The LAN Manager   61
   Helping Users   63
   Upgrades   63
   File Management   64
   Backup   65
   Usage   66
   Security   66
   Spooling   67
   User Support   68
   Additional Resources   70

8 Maintenance and Troubleshooting   **71**

   Support   71
   Prevention   73
   Response   74
   Typical Problems   75
   Conclusion   79
   Additional Resources   79

9 Advanced Capabilities   **81**

   Programming   81
   Mac vs. PC   83
   Server Specialization   84
   Other Effects   85
   Virtual Libraries   86
   Additional Resources   88

10 Connections 89

    Asynchronous Communications 91
    CD-ROM Access 92
    Internet Connections 93
    Other Technologies 94
    Conclusion 95
    Additional Resources 96

11 LANs in Labs 97

    Setting Up a Lab 97
    Software Environment 99
    Policy Planning 100
    Additional Resources 101

Afterword 103

Appendixes 105

A   Library Needs Analysis Form 105
B   User Needs Profile 107
C   LAN Operating System Environmental Profile 109
D   System Reliability: Checking Hardware and
       Software Features 111
E   Disk Space Estimation Form 113
F   Network Backup Procedure 115
G   Topologies 117
H   Wiring Survey 121
I   Selecting Library Systems 125
J   Sample User Account Information Form 127
K   Sample Job Description 129
L   Checklist for Major Upgrades 133
M Equipment Maintenance Record Form 135
N   Sample Virus Policy Statement 137
O   Glossary 139

Index 145

Colophon 147

FIGURES

2.1   Directory Structure   16
5.1   Categorizing Applications Software   44
6.1   Login Process Relationships   58

Appendix A   Library Needs Analysis Form   105
Appendix B   User Needs Profile   107
Appendix C   LAN Operating System Environmental
              Profile   109
Appendix D   System Reliability: Checking Hardware
              and Software Features   111
Appendix E   Disk Space Estimation Form   113
Appendix F   Network Backup Procedure   115
Appendix G   Topologies   117
Appendix H   Wiring Survey   121
Appendix I   Selecting Library Systems   125
Appendix J   Sample User Account Information Form   127
Appendix K   Sample Job Description—Local Area Network
              Manager   129
Appendix L   Checklist for Major Upgrades   133
Appendix M   Equipment Maintenance Record Form   135
Appendix N   Sample Virus Policy Statement   137

PREFACE

Libraries today are in the throes of adapting to new computer and communication systems that were only beginning to be implemented when the first edition of this book was written five years ago. We have new choices to make between accessing locally held and remote resources. Communication with colleagues in other regions and on other continents has become routine. Yet the network world is still growing through national and state initiatives; networking of rural areas and intranets are two "home-based" issues of the moment. More libraries must face the task of planning and building their own electronic infrastructures and achieving the necessary understanding of the technological processes required. *Local Area Networking for the Small Library* is an introduction to those processes and the planning necessary to begin purchasing, installing, and implementing these new systems.

I assume that you know something about the computers you are currently using. If you are using an operating system like MS-DOS, the Macintosh system, Windows 3.1, Windows 95, or OS/2 to run your computer, you can build from there. If you have doubts, keep your computer manuals handy to clarify what I am talking about.

Local Area Networking for the Small Library: A How-to-Do-It Manual has two main parts. The first part, Chapters 1 through 5, introduces the ingredients needed to build a local area network (LAN). The second part, Chapters 6 through 11, explores the problems of operating a LAN. Each chapter features practical tips so you can achieve your objective to learn about setting up a LAN in the library. If you are going to be doing some of the technical tasks, whether ordering equipment or installing the system, it will be useful to start from Chapter 1 and read straight through. If, however, you are a manager and will be directing someone else to set up the system, you should probably begin with the section in Chapter 7 about LAN manager responsibilities first.

This second edition incorporates many changes from the first edition. These include

- expanded and updated discussions of both the technical and public service aspects of planning and implementing CD-ROM networks
- a comparison of the various available network operating systems as they are utilized in typical library settings
- additional specifications and considerations for LANs that support online catalog systems

- more information about and practical tips for setting up individual library employee and public user workstations
- updated bibliographies at the end of each chapter
- discussions throughout the book of the steps necessary for making the Internet and the World Wide Web accessible via the library's LAN

Regardless of the road that brought you to consider building a LAN, remember that this is a grass-roots phenomenon. Networks of personal computers build on a tradition of user independence, innovation, and decentralization. This book is for those who cannot afford expensive mistakes, but who are genuinely interested in progress, and who are open minded enough to seek advice. After reading the book, readers will be able to plan, implement, secure, and maintain local area networks that both facilitate basic networking functions and incorporate CD-ROM and communication servers in their libraries. These networks comprise your own library's information infrastructure which can both enable your own computers to share information and your users and staff to connect to the Internet from any connected personal computer.

Turn the page to see if you recognize your library in any of the opening scenarios.

1 WHAT IS A LAN?

In the innovative company executives do not say, "This is a damn-fool idea." Instead they ask, "What would be needed to make this embryonic, half-baked, foolish idea into something that makes sense, that is feasible, that is an opportunity for us?"

Peter F. Drucker
The Frontiers of Management

When you want to print a letter on the secretary's laser printer, do you have to put on your sneakers and carry a diskette to the secretary? If several staff members work on a database in dBASE, must they get together weekly to share updates? Do patrons complain about having to wait in line for a terminal with a printer?

Local area networks help eliminate these inconveniences associated with sharing resources among many microcomputers. They may do a great deal more, of course, including making CD-ROMs accessible, providing links to departments outside the library, and making work groups more productive. But when you first ask a group of people what they want, sharing printers, sharing software, and sharing data are certain to be high on the list.

Physically, a local area network (LAN) is a collection of wiring that links one central computer to many workstation computers distributed around the organization. But LANs can be surprisingly complex because so much of what makes the LAN effective is software that hides invisibly "under the skin" of the hardware.

Before considering what you need to build a LAN, let's examine our assumptions about how a LAN fits into a library or information center. From a user perspective, libraries are agencies for putting people in contact with information, usually by providing subject access. From a staff perspective, libraries are also work groups with a service orientation. Both staff and users have needs that constrain their use of automation. Users need access to information in as convenient a manner as possible. The work group needs to share access to common facilities such as the catalog. Work-group members need to coordinate their activities with each other, as when they refer a patron from one person or department to another. Reference librarians who are locked into attending a desk need to communicate with people in other departments and with fellow reference librarians on other work shifts.

These needs constrain the nature of a LAN in several ways. A LAN with a central computer or "server" can best handle a variety of tasks and provide the simplest means of managing a complex environment. If library software is operated on the LAN, the server can handle shared files for circulation and the online catalog. A server-based system can provide the best assurance of forwarding mail messages to people not currently using the system and can handle the multiple communication interfaces to support users conveniently. These constraints leave a wide variety of hardware, software, and operating system options to consider.

Beyond the obvious ways that libraries work, it is clear that they are professional organizations. Support for management functions that will yield useful statistical data, security systems to protect privacy, and communication systems that facilitate collegiality are all vital tasks to be performed by a LAN.

COMPONENTS

A list of the ingredients for a LAN must include hardware, software, power supply, wiring, data storage devices, special interfaces, and workstation cards. A preliminary list might look like this:

- computer to act as a server
    - memory of at least 16 megabytes
    - operating system software
    - hard disk of at least one gigabyte
    - server network interface card
    - interface card to other systems
- network-compatible applications programs
- usage monitoring software
- virus protection software
- e-mail/desktop software
- uninterruptible power supply for the server
- network cards for workstations that will be attached to the LAN
- cabling and connectors
- wiring hubs, signal boosters, and other units required to complete the cabling and connection to other systems
- printer(s) for central use and spooling software, if required
- telecommunications hardware for attaching to an organizational backbone or to an Internet provider

These components are typical for most LANs, but there is much more involved in structuring an individual installation. Each LAN has to be built to meet the needs of the particular departments and groups of people that it will serve. Forms that can be used to assess organizational and user needs are provided in Appendixes A and B.

LAN OPERATIONS

In a library there are typically three environments likely to be incorporated into the operations of a LAN. First, there are library operations such as circulation, the online catalog or database, acquisitions, and serials. Second are the administrative processes of the library including budgeting, personnel, training, and management processes (planning, organizing, directing, and controlling). Third are the ancillary services of a library, particularly microcomputer labs, media centers, and self-service facilities.

These three functions—library operations, administration, and ancillary services—more than likely will operate on the same LAN when the system is first set up. As databases and functions grow, each may develop to the point of requiring a dedicated server.

LANs for library operations must be woven into the fabric of the organization. Like "enterprise-wide" systems in business, the primary purpose is to implement a system that serves all aspects of the organization. Such software is provided by many vendors and will ideally include circulation, the online catalog, acquisitions, and serials control. Many systems will also have the capability to perform management and ancillary functions.

Not to be forgotten at the planning stage is support for the library user. To connect users, most libraries will consider tying the LAN in to parent organization systems, providing dial-up access, or providing Internet access—or all three. Techniques for setting up such connections are discussed in Chapter 10. As you begin to think about a LAN, keep in mind the ultimate goal of serving users better.

An important consideration for the small library in planning an online library system is whether an "integrated" library system or one with independent functions is required. This is a difficult decision for the small library and the issue goes well beyond the scope of planning for a LAN. It is important, however, to regard this issue from the viewpoint of the library and what must be done to serve user needs best.

LIBRARY OPERATIONS

Ideally, the online catalog used by the library should be closely allied with the acquisitions and circulation systems so that record need be entered only once when material is ordered. Records are then made available as catalog entries and circulation master records. The possible drawbacks of having one encompassing system may lie within the library operations software and how well that software will support users who are not in the library. Is the catalog access sufficiently "user friendly" that a remote user can make it work without complex user aids? Does the integrated library software limit the number of concurrent users? Is the catalog software efficient enough that when multiple users access the system it will provide rapid response without bogging down?

Should the answers to some of these questions require an alternative solution, it may be reasonable to consider an information storage and retrieval system (ISAR). Small libraries, such as law libraries, whose operational emphasis is on subject access rather than on circulation, may find such systems a solution. There is an important tradeoff. A retrieval system allows for shorter bibliographic records since MARC records are not required, but there is a limitation in upgrade options. If records in a retrieval system are not formatted to be compatible with the MARC record, it may only be possible to upgrade to another retrieval system—unless the library is willing to invest in custom programming or data conversion. On the other hand, some retrieval system vendors, such as INMAGIC and ProCite, offer optional utility programs for downloading MARC records from such databases as DIALOG and OCLC. They may also offer the capability of exporting in MARC format.

Library operations software, also called an integrated online library system (IOLS), may require a dedicated server immediately. It is the nature of these systems to require large files with multiple index files for subject access. The program may assume that it "owns" a disk drive when it is installed. If that is the case, the system may not work (or may not work as well) if other applications reside on the same hard disk. This is less of a problem with modern, nationally advertised software.

Software vendors often offer LAN hardware and operating system packages as an option for their systems. Libraries should be particularly cautious in acquiring a system in this manner. Questions that should be asked include: Is the operating system provided by the vendor a "mainstream" operating system that will be compatible with other systems and applications software? Is the protocol used for transmission (e.g., Ethernet, Arcnet) one for which workstation interface cards will be available for the variety of microcomputers that the library may come to own? Is the protocol hospitable to CD-ROM servers that the library will grow into? Is the operating system software provided by the vendor a current version?

While an outdated or less compatible system may provide somewhat greater initial reliability and ease of installation, it may unduly restrict library growth. One important consideration may be that operating system vendors offer less expensive upgrades to owners of previous versions of their software. If the version provided by a library software vendor is too old, the library may have to pay full price rather just purchasing an upgrade. Another consideration in choosing a vendor-supplied system is that the technology used in the LAN may not be the same as that of the library's parent institution. If there is no compatibility, the library may be unable to avail itself of parent institution technical support that is already in place.

Is upgrading the operating system essential? The answer, usually, is yes. Applications software often requires an operating system of some minimum version level to match its abilities. Interface connection software to parent institution systems may also be upgraded and demand operating system upgrades in order to continue to function.

ADMINISTRATIVE APPLICATIONS

Not to be forgotten in the matrix of operational tasks is the need for workgroup productivity tools that can be economically served from the LAN. Generic applications like word processors, spreadsheets, and databases are strong and useful throughout the library. Libraries are graduating from typewriters and calculators to microcomputers. The flexibility and productivity of microcomputer software is well understood. In a LAN environment, networked software provides a standard across the library that insures that all can communicate ideas and plans with ease.

Productivity applications also encompass a wide variety of software for tying the work group together and for providing workstations with a "desktop" environment. Such applications may provide menus for novices, calculators, electronic mail, calendar and scheduling programs, notebook databases, and telephone dialers. All the library staff, professionals and paraprofessionals alike, will be able to solve problems faster and coordinate their activities better with such tools. Managers will find that rapport with colleagues and subordinates improves and fewer misunderstandings occur when communications are well documented in e-mail messages.

Library administration is not neglected in a LAN. Unlike other systems, however, there is no dedicated software unless you count work-group productivity software and statistical software. Spreadsheet software may suffice for many small libraries, but the major statistical programs like SPSS and SAS are also available for installation on LANs.

The key ingredient that transforms generic software into management software is ingenuity. A spreadsheet is commonly viewed as primarily a tool for analysis, but many LAN users have found that setting up "round-robin" transmissions of budgets is a time-saver. The library director can format an outline budget, then transmit it as an e-Mail attachment to each professional or department in the library. Each unit can add its own figures to the spreadsheet, perform individual "what if" scenarios, and keep a copy for file. The amended copy is returned for aggregation into a master budget which will be replete with detailed notations about variable costs and program justifications.

Some microcomputer opportunities are also management nightmares. One that is a special problem in libraries is the duplication of databases between departments. A LAN can solve this problem by centralizing database files in one directory on the server. In this situation it is easier for departments to be aware of each others' activities. Input to a shared database is very feasible and makes resource sharing possible within many library organizations that are geographically fragmented.

Supervision and coordination are important management functions that can be greatly facilitated in a LAN environment. Managers can interact with all of their subordinates, developing budgets, planning, and discussing projects on a daily basis. The LAN makes the manager a presence in every subordinate work center without taking large amounts of time. Remote work centers also have better contact with the manager.

Another management process, training, is easily coordinated in a LAN environment. Notices of training opportunities can be handled informally by the director using electronic mail, or they can be handled formally, using a scheduling program. In a microcomputer environment, training can actually be distributed over the LAN through menus that connect to electronic tutorials, enabling novices to access the training they need easily and progress in a manner that matches their abilities and interests.

ANCILLARY SERVICES

Specialized ancillary services of libraries face rather different problems in using a LAN. Microcomputer labs, media centers, and self-service operations demand special physical layouts and unusual software. Microcomputer labs and media centers with many workstations need to be structured so that wiring for electricity and the LAN are kept out of the way of users. One way to accomplish this is with wiring channels built into furnishings. A newer way is to use alternative cabling techniques such as flatwire that goes beneath the carpet or wireless systems that use infrared or radio technology.

Software used in labs and media centers should include something like LanAssist that will allow the instructor or coordinator to "look over the shoulder" of users. Such software allows the instructor to see the user's screen and perform keyboard actions as though the instructor were at the student workstation. Software is also available that allows the instructor to highlight items on the screen to demonstrate solutions to the student.

A key consideration in lab and media settings is the compatibility of hardware and software. It is most helpful for all students to have identical keyboards and monitors, even though CPUs and hard disks may differ. Also, the software used to "look over their shoulders" works best when everything is the same.

Another ancillary service with increasing electronic presence is interlibrary loan (ILL). Some integrated packages have an ILL component and there are also standalone ILL software packages. Such software primarily benefits the librarian by providing order tracking for ILL requests. In a LAN environment, users become accustomed to desktop interaction with services that previously required the users' physical presence in the library. Many library systems have instituted ILL access from the user workstation. It is a simple matter to develop an ILL form in a word processor format or in a programming language such as BASIC or C. Where users have individual LAN accounts, they may be uniquely identified for billing purposes. Bringing new services like this to the user greatly enhances library visibility and credibility.

PLANNING

Microcomputers, like any computing system, can pose pitfalls for the unwary. Many microcomputer users work with systems set up and maintained by others. They are often unaware of the system responsibilities that fall to the user—until some inconvenient or catastrophic event occurs. Proper planning for the setup and continued operation of a LAN will insure that when problems arise, solutions are swift and inconvenience to users is minimal.

Planning should begin with a commitment from the library's management or the parent institution. It is important to have defined the LAN's primary task, even though it will facilitate many other tasks. By establishing the primary task, it is possible to focus programmatic and budgetary resources on the LAN project.

The second step is to gain some familiarity with the literature. The library should have a subscription to general purpose microcomputer magazines, to a LAN magazine, and to some of the free vendor-supported journals in data communications and LAN technology. By keeping up with new product announcements and current trends in technology, you will be prepared to make good purchasing decisions for the LAN. This would be the best time to appoint the LAN manager. Since the LAN manager must operate and maintain the system when it is set up, his or her involvement at an early stage and commitment to the implementation plan are essential.

The third step in planning a LAN is to assess the environment in which it will be placed. Where in the facility can a server be located? What connections to other computer systems will be needed? Will new workstations be required for some users? How ready are users to take advantage of the computing resources that will be at their disposal? Help with finding answers to these questions can be found in later chapters on hardware, wiring, start up, and operations.

Fourth, plan the hardware and software environment that will meet the needs of management and users. This includes choosing an operating system, hardware, applications software, and utility software required to operate and maintain the LAN.

The fifth step is to plan the site for the LAN. Choose a location, determine physical security, make printer locations accessible, and locate shelving for LAN documentation. A cabling survey must be performed to determine where installers can run cables and what obstacles must be surmounted. Electrical connections for the server and workstations must be correctly located and must supply appropriate power levels. The result of this step will be work orders to the physical-plant department or a purchase order to a LAN installation and wiring contractor.

Next you will specify the necessary hardware, software, and accessories. Institutional policies concerning purchasing vary tremendously, but certain general procedures should be followed. First, compatibility should be specified wherever possible. The components of the system must be compatible with the planned topology and transmission protocol of the LAN. Software must work with the personal computers that will make up the system. Hubs, routers, and switches must be compatible with the LAN and the other systems to which they connect. Second, minimal performance standards should be specified if possible. LAN hardware and software, for example, make it possible for you to specify a minimum data-transmission speed. Backup tapes and hard disks have specified data-transfer rates. Software has some limitations on file size and number of records. Requiring compatibility and performance criteria helps insure that you will receive the quality materials needed to establish an effective LAN.

IMPLEMENTATION

Installation is next. If someone in your organization has experience installing LANs you should ask for that person's advice and assistance during installation. Some or all of the installation tasks may be contracted, providing the library supervises the contractor to insure that all essential tasks are completed and that documentation of the LAN configuration is obtained.

Implementation of the LAN—flipping the switch, so to speak— is not the last step. You will initially turn the system on as soon as the minimum components are available. This is important because you want to establish that everything works while it is still under warranty. You will probably want to identify a few knowledgeable users who can use the system immediately and help you simulate intense use situations.

The final step is training the users. Training can actually commence as soon as you have a commitment to installing a LAN, because there are likely to be some users who need to learn basic things about computers and about the operating system of their workstations before they will feel comfortable with the LAN. As soon as applications software is selected, training can begin. Ideally, training for applications that run on the LAN should take place in a LAN environment. You may be able to find a neighboring organization with a similar LAN and applications, or you may have to hire someone to do training. Library software vendors usually offer onsite training packages for their products.

Once you complete an initial backup-to-tape of all the data on the server, you enter the next phase of the LAN life cycle: daily operations. LANs tend to have a dynamic life cycle because most users have no experience from which to project new needs and uses that will affect the system. At a minimum, it is usually wise to expect that some new major component will be added to the system every 18 months. You may need more storage and thus may go to a larger hard disk. A new version of the operating system may become available. You may need to replace printers. Wiring may develop faults. An increase in the number of users may dictate migration to a faster server. LAN managers learn that change is a way of life, and good managers plan for change. Proper data backups are needed. Documentation of the system configuration is needed. Most important, close observation of system integrity and performance is needed. Provide a LAN manager the time and support he or she will need to do a good job.

ADDITIONAL RESOURCES

Angier, Jennifer J., and Susan B. Hoehl. "Local Area Networks (LAN) in the Special Library: Part 1—A Planning Model." *Online* (November 1986): 19–28. Provides a good example of the planning and problem solving necessary in choosing a network.

Flower, Eric, and Lisa Thulstrup. "Setting Up a Public Use Local Area Network." *Wilson Library Bulletin* 63(September 1988):45–47. Addresses specific issues for librarians.

Hoehl, Susan B. "Local Area Networks: Effective Tools for Special Libraries." *Online* (September 1988): 64–68.

Hoehl, Susan B., and Jennifer J. Angier. "Local Area Networks (LAN) in the Special Library: Part 2—Implementation." *Online* (November 1986): 29–36.

Kemper, Marilyn. *Networking: Choosing a LAN Path to Interconnection.* Metuchen, N.J.: The Scarecrow Press, 1987. A classic—offers a strong starting point for understanding early networking, much of which is still in place.

Leggott, Mark. "Local Area Networks—For Your Library?" *Canadian Library Journal* 46(October 1989):303–305.

Levert, Virginia M. "Applications of Local Area Networks of Microcomputers in Libraries." *Information Technology and Libraries* 4(March 1985):9–18. Gives a mainstream explanation of what LANs are good for.

Matthews, Joseph R., and Mark R. Porer. "Local Area Networks or LANs." *Library Technology Reports.* 31(January–February 1995): 5–110.

Nemzow, Martin. *Keeping the Link: Ethernet Installation and Management.* New York: McGraw-Hill, 1988. Provides technical information that will make putting wires in place a lot easier.

Weidlin, James R., and Thomas B. Cross. *Networking Personal Computers in Organizations.* Homewood, Ill.: Dow Jones-Irwin, 1986. Offers the important viewpoints about why networking is done. An older but thorough treatment.

2 OPERATING SYSTEMS

In this game of high adventure, your object is to travel 200 miles across the great Gobi Desert. You're being chased by a tribe of knock-kneed pygmies. You have one quart of water which will last you for six drinks; it may be renewed if you find an oasis or, if you are found by another traveler, you may get an additional half-quart of water. During your journey you may encounter all types of hazards such as sand storms, wild Berbers and possible injuries to your camel.

David H. Ahl
Basic Computer Games

The choice of a LAN operating system may well be driven by the choice of library applications software. Vendors may provide versions of their library systems for different workstation operating systems, but it will be up to you to ask which LAN operating systems are compatible with their software. Choose wisely; as in David Ahl's traveler, it's a long journey between oases.

The operating system of your LAN will largely dictate what users can do. Ability to perform basic tasks such as printing and sending electronic mail is often determined by the operating system.

An operating system performs functions in four major categories: file management, data transmission, printer spooling, and message transmission. File management is the most complex function and is the cornerstone of network activity from a user's perspective.

LAN operating systems may or may not operate from a system server. Systems with servers are termed server-based; systems without servers are termed peer-to-peer networks. Server-based systems have an inherent advantage in that they allow secure file sharing, and, most important, software sharing. Peer-to-peer systems generally require applications software to be installed on each workstation—a considerable expense. At this point, peer-to-peer systems without servers have been relegated to the smallest, less mainstream niches.

When the server is booted, the operating system itself is loaded and then some of the large amount of available memory is used as buffer space. As users call for applications to be run on their workstations, the server loads the applications into memory. It keeps in memory the applications and files that are most frequently demanded. In this way the server minimizes wear and tear on the hard disk by reading the disk a minimum number of times.

Files stored on the server's hard disk can be made available to groups of users or to individuals. Libraries of clip-art graphics,

11

administrative forms, report formats, mailing lists, supply inventories, and bibliographies can be centrally maintained but remotely accessed. Users who work on common projects but on different aspects of them (such as budgets, publicity flyers, or user aids) can share files and use the LAN as their assembly line.

The other tasks performed by the server—data transmission, message transmission, and printer spooling—all use the server's disk storage as part of the process of moving data from one point to another. Data transmission is simply the task of moving files from workstations to the server or from the server to other systems outside the LAN. Message transmission involves moving mail through the LAN while maintaining security for the transmission. Message transmission usually includes the ability to send a message immediately to any logged-in user. Printer spooling is the process of storing the content of print jobs that are en route to a printer. This process also usually involves routing the print jobs, which may include transmission to a printer outside the workgroup LAN.

In addition to these principal tasks, the server performs a variety of support functions. Vendors offer "value added processes" (VAPs) which are software programs that run on the server. One VAP may provide a database program, another may provide mail service, and yet another may allow unusual types of workstations to connect with the server. Novell uses "NetWare Loadable Modules" (NLMs) in more recent versions. NLMs improve memory management on the server; the advantage of NLMs is that they can be loaded or unloaded without taking the server "down" or offline.

COMPATIBILITY

The first step in selecting a LAN operating system is to assess the compatibilities required and the user workstations to be supported. An analysis form is included in Appendix C. This form does not answer the question "Which operating system shall I buy?" but it advises you to consider some important variables in making that decision.

Operating systems for LANs come in four "flavors":

- disk operating system (DOS)/Windows compatible
- Apple Macintosh compatible
- UNIX compatible
- OS/2 compatible

These "flavors" include a wide variety of operating systems. The spectrum of systems includes varying degrees of technological sophistication and price.

DOS-compatible network operating systems cover a wide variety of topologies and operating systems. They are intended to support workstations operating MS-DOS, PC-DOS, and Windows, although other workstation operating systems have begun to be supported. Four vendors stand out: Novell, Banyan, IBM, and Microsoft. Each has a significant share of the LAN market and has stayed abreast of developments in the industry. Each operating system will work with certain protocols, topologies, and types of wiring. It is wise to obtain vendor specifications before planning your system wiring. Windows as a network system has several versions, including Windows for Workgroups and Windows NT. The competition between Microsoft Windows and Novell NetWare is one of the most interesting in the field. So far Novell has retained dominance both in functionality and the marketplace, but the competition is serious and the choices are not easy. Recent reviews have focused on the ease of administration, difficulty of installation, use of directory services, and integration.

Banyan's Vines operating system is an interesting product with roots in the UNIX environment. It has been particularly well received in areas where compatibility with larger computer systems is important. The Vines strong point is its "naming service" which allows directory service interface to external mail systems. This feature is important when users on the LAN want their electronic mail systems to send messages to users on mainframe systems or to connect to Bitnet.

IBM has been a strong player in the LAN world, introducing token-ring systems that work with proprietary operating systems as well as with Novell. The IBM token-ring operating system was initially a peer-to-peer system that operated primarily with proprietary hardware. As it has evolved, it has included a server capability and, like many IBM products, has been folded into several products to become all things to all people. Democratization of the marketplace has forced token-ring into focus more as a topology than as an operating system, since Novell will run on token ring. Major hardware vendors such as IBM, Compaq, and DEC are resellers for Novell products. If your parent organization has invested heavily in a particular brand of hardware products, you may need to examine compatibility issues to determine whether the Novell software accommodates specific features of your hardware vendor's system. If the operating system has been adapted in some way, you should purchase the version that the hardware vendor supplies.

AppleTalk is a peer-to-peer network that works primarily with Apple computers. Interface cards for other computers, including IBM PC–compatible systems, are available from third-party vendors. The system is intended to connect workstations with each other or with an AppleTalk server. Where Internet connectivity is needed, it will be necessary to have a Macintosh Ethernet card and to operate TCP/IP drivers with the most recent version of the operating system. AppleTalk servers provide file storage and software storage. The fact that AppleTalk uses unshielded twisted-pair wire was a distinct advantage when first introduced, but most network protocols now accommodate twisted-pair wire.

UNIX operating system, which has been around for over twenty years, was originated by Ken Thompson at the Bell Labs. It is a powerful system that is essentially a down-sized minicomputer operating system, offering a strong macro-language that puts DOS-based systems to shame. Vendors such as Sun Microsystems and Silicon Graphics (SGI) have used UNIX to build sophisticated systems for industrial users. AT&T and advanced workstation makers offer UNIX as a standard option; Intel-based computers may use a version of Berkeley UNIX or LINUX, a shareware version. UNIX provides full service to users, including security, printer sharing, and messaging.

The OS/2-compatible operating systems are produced and distributed by IBM. LAN Manager provides support both for advanced workstations operating under OS/2 and older workstations operating under DOS. Since a core group of at least six powerful workstations would provide the impetus for investing in such a system, a LAN Manager network is likely to be a pricey high-end project. These systems represent the leading edge of programming technology, so LAN planners should at least watch their development carefully.

SYSTEM ORGANIZATION

What does a LAN operating system look like? It can be difficult to look at someone else's concept of an operating system interface and determine what buttons to push or how to give commands. Fortunately, some basic analogies or metaphors are relevant in most modern computer systems. One of these is based on the fact that a large hard-disk storage system must be subdivided into manageable units called subdirectories. The process of subdividing the disk yields a structure shaped like the branching roots of a tree. Another metaphor used with DOS is the notion of paths that note a route among the subdirectories. By formally noting certain paths, the user may designate to the operating system where to look for executable files (programs). In the operating system, the paths may be designated with a shorthand that uses the alphabetical letters for disk drives to map out the paths (see Figure 2–1).

Users may or may not see the drive mappings, depending upon their level of expertise and how thoroughly the LAN manager chooses to protect them from their environment. LAN managers used to "wall off" users from the unadorned LAN operating system environment by embedding users in a menu system, but now there are graphical interfaces that control the desktop environment. Maintenance of the workstation graphics interface has become an important issue within the network operating system environment. It takes time and skill to install, configure, maintain, and upgrade the individual workstations. LAN managers now put effort into tracking the configuration of workstations, maintaining as much uniformity as possible, and using centralized methods for managing workstations.

SECURITY

The features that a server-based LAN provides can exist only if the LAN operating system has a reliable environment. This is made possible by the user security protocols and secure file environment provided by the operating system. LANs could not function with merely workstation-level security, where the user can easily, and even accidentally, erase all of the files on disk storage.

LAN security is usually provided in three ways: by user login accounts, by file access limitations, and by directory access limitations. Directory access controls are the most important feature, for with them admission to an entire directory structure can be limited by specific rules. Typically, access rules limit the user's ability to search directories, create files, delete files, or create subordinate directories.

Security access limits for files can be controlled by a variety of parameters. The Novell operating system makes a good example. In this system, files can be set to "EXECUTE ONLY" (no write access), so that a program can be executed but the file containing the program can not be deleted or overwritten. Other parameters control whether a file can be read, written, modified, or deleted.

Figure 2–1: Directory Structure

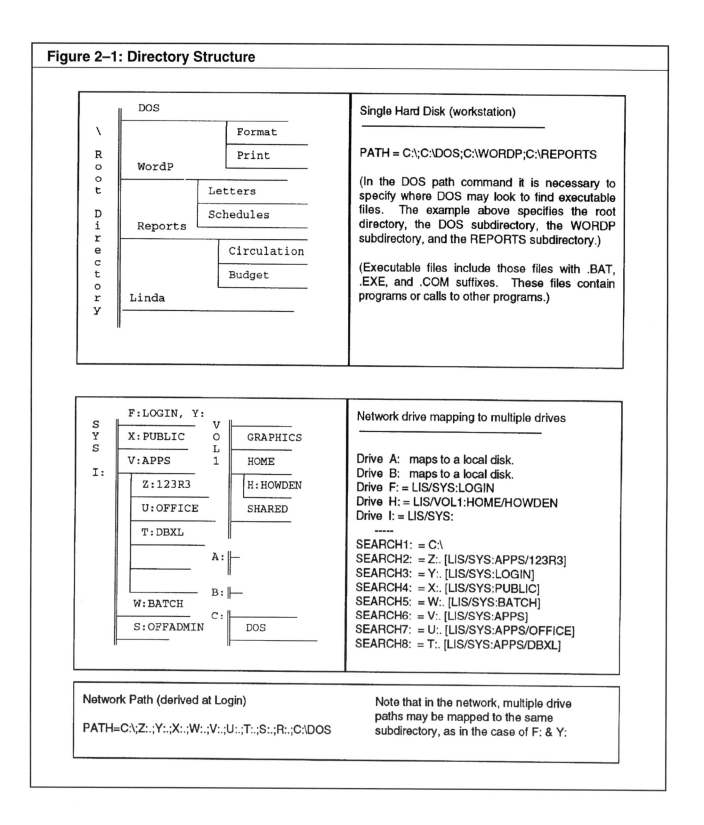

These security parameters also serve as a first line of defense against virus attacks, since few programmers have the knowledge to circumvent LAN security procedures. Files can also be hidden so that their names do not appear in the directory.

Libraries will find both the protection provided by security features and the flexibility of those features very important. When library users access services provided through the LAN, even simple mistakes are potential major problems. Many libraries provide e-mail, CD-ROM, or Internet access, and for such purposes public users often need server workspace that is securely separate from other applications and from staff users.

STANDARDS

Operating systems for LANs are not standardized by the way they work internally, but rather in their manner of operation with workstations and with each other. The communication of signals within a LAN has been standardized to the extent that there is an international standard, the Open Systems Interconnection (OSI) model, for LAN operation. This model provides sufficient standardization to allow connection of different vendors' hardware within the same network. Standards continue to evolve with the technology. Unlike standardization in some other areas, networking standards often precede widespread introduction of new products. The standardization process often serves as a forum for negotiation and competition between manufacturers. Keeping an eye on standardization news may help you understand which technologies are worth investing in, which are obsolescent, and which are risky.

The evolution of electronic protocols is somewhat serendipitous. Industrial and professional groups provide arenas for discussing and promulgating standards. The marketplace, government procurement requirements, and coalitions of producers influence the direction of technological development. Clearly, the market has forced a democratization of LAN technology because it is in everyone's best interest to have some standard protocols available that allow most systems to connect with each other. Currently the most widely used protocols are OSI and IEEE 802 compatible. While standards may change, the rule of sticking with the most widely available standards is a good one.

SYSTEMS FEATURES

What features should you look for in purchasing a LAN operating system? We can list those that are essential and those that might be useful. Many others might be nice to have.

Essential features:

- security that protects both files and directories
- drivers for the interface cards that will work with each type of workstation that the library owns
- bridge options that will accommodate remote sites if the library has branches
- batch file capabilities where operating system commands can be used as a macro language and stored in a file for execution as a task script
- ability to work with the transmission protocol (e.g., Ethernet, Arcnet) that the LAN will use
- printer spooling
- drivers for hard disks with a capacity greater than one gigabyte
- ability to run on advanced microcomputers and to utilize large amounts of memory effectively

Useful features:

- ability to work with another protocol used by workstations that have unique LAN protocols (e.g., AppleTalk)
- support for higher level messaging systems
- menu or "desktop" software that allows users to locate and launch application programs easily
- usage tracking that creates a record of users and the amount of connect time and computing activity
- support for HSM (hierarchical storage management) that allows the operating system to transfer less-used data to rewriteable CD-ROM or to backup tape without operator intervention
- availability of drivers to support advanced LAN communication protocols, including ATM (asynchronous transfer mode), FDDI/CDDI, or other 100 Mbps (megabytes per second) protocols.

SUB-LANS

Cheaper solutions offer themselves as work-group solutions for small offices. If your budget is tight you may be tempted to try them. What are the pros and cons of "sub-LANS"?

Arguments in favor of sub-LANs are that they are inexpensive, they provide file and printer sharing, and users can install them. If your requirements are entirely administrative and if they fit within the services provided, a sub-LAN may suit your needs.

The arguments against sub-LANs are that they may not connect to other LANs in the parent organization; workstations with different operating systems can not be accommodated; applications software can not be shared; there may not be a common server for file sharing; and there may be no ability to define user accounts for security purposes. Growth is usually out of the question. Enlarging the number of workstations served beyond about six usually requires new LAN interface cards or a new operating system or both. If LAN-capable library software is to be used, sub-LANs probably will not work with those packages.

UTILITIES

Operating systems come with a wide variety of features, many of which only a LAN manager will appreciate. One feature that even a novice can appreciate is the procedure that allows a new user to be defined to the operating system. Important questions that need to be asked about such a procedure include

- Is the procedure to create new users done through menu-driven software?
- Are user passwords accessible to the LAN manager after the account has been established? (They should not be.)
- Are there provisions for creating groups of users with equivalent security?
- Are there parameters for controlling the time of day a user accesses the system and the amount of disk space available to the user?

Another utility that should be available in an operating system is the procedure for printer spooling. Printing is one of the LAN's primary tasks, so its capability to facilitate printing is a priority consideration. At the very least, the LAN operating system should allow print jobs to be stored (buffered or spooled) en route to a printer connected to the server. It is very desirable to control the print process, and one way to do this is to specify print job priorities for certain users or groups of users. Another desirable feature is the ability to create multiple "queues" or waiting lines for printers. Commands that allow real-time management of printing should be available at the server (the system console) or at an operator's workstation. The operator should be able to cancel or restart print jobs and to check on the status of printers and jobs.

PURCHASED UTILITIES

Additional utilities may be supplied by other software. In addition to virus-check software and backup programs, a LAN may need a software license tracking program, management software, or a remote installation program.

An important facility for conserving resources is a software package that will allow you to monitor usage of applications software. Most applications software does not have usage monitoring built in. Thus it is possible for more users to utilize the software simultaneously than you have licenses for. By adding a monitoring system you can record daily usage for trends and you can automatically prevent unlicensed usage. Statistics can also be collected about use of library software, if the program can report specific workstations or user categories. Lab users need metering, too, to identify which applications are used the most.

LAN management software is a complicated field, but there are some good uses for these packages. The better programs use simple network management protocol (SNMP) to talk with peripheral devices in the system. This software allows you to check the status of remote intelligent hubs, workstation cards, and other devices—without trekking from office to office around the organization. Some problems, such as network cards set to improper addresses, are most easily diagnosed with such software. Although not absolutely essential, LAN management software should be considered if downtime or troubleshooting time is likely to be embarrassing for the library.

Remote installation programs are used to set up software on a workstation without actually going to the workstation. Such programs do have limitations, but they can save a lot of time. Even if most applications are stored on a server, there will be a need to upgrade workstation LAN drivers and virus checkers. A clever LAN manager can do a remote installation using batch files, but there are limitations, particularly with troubleshooting, to what can be done in this way.

Take the time to give full consideration to the operating system you purchase. It is the key ingredient that can make or break all of the effort that you put into LAN development. Users may never appreciate many of the conveniences a good operating system provides, but they certainly will not appreciate lack of compatibility and inadequate functionality in a poor one.

ADDITIONAL RESOURCES

Currid, Cheryl C. *Novell's Guide to NetWare 4.0 Networks*. San Jose, Calif.: Novell Press, 1993.

Darling, Charles B. "Is It Time to Change your NOS?" *Datamation* 41(September 1, 1995):71–73.

Duffy, Carolina A. "Who Got the Other 25 percent?" *PC Week*, 12(January 30, 1995):1. Describes market share split between Novell and Microsoft.

Giorgis, Tadesse W. "Networks for the Enterprise." *Byte* 20(February 1995): 119–128.

Lipschutz, Robert P., et al. "The Versatile Network Operating System." *PC Magazine* 14(May 30, 1995): 228–258. Includes benchmark tests.

Madron, Thomas W. *Local Area Networks: New Technologies, Emerging Standards. 3rd ed.* New York: Wiley, 1994.

Moriera, Paula. *Novell's Guide to NetWare Management*, Alameda, Calif.: Sypbex, 1995.

Siyan, Karanjit. *NetWare: The Professional Reference*. 3rd ed. Indianapolis: New Riders Publishing, 1994.

3 HARDWARE

Computer systems are not gods. They are very fallible and must be designed to survive all sorts of terrible events. They may not continue running when the lights go out, but they must not lose the data recorded up to the time of the power failure.

R. J. Braithwaite
Proceedings of the 1978 Clinic on
Library Applications of Data Processing

Hardware for a LAN normally includes

- server
- direct access storage devices (DASD—hard disk drives)
- workstations
- LAN interface cards for the server and workstations
- printer(s)
- interface cards to other networks
- uninterruptible power supply
- tape backup system
- LAN manager's workstation
- security devices

SERVER

The key hardware unit in most information center LANs will be a powerful high-speed microcomputer used as a server—the heart of the system. It will be equipped with a large amount of memory and a high-capacity hard disk. In the world of LAN servers there are two types of microcomputer systems: those that are specialized units and those that are off-the-shelf high-speed workstation units.

Specialized servers are those that have some particular architecture that makes them more efficient in a LAN role. Such features include more bays for disk drives, multiple large power supplies, multiple high-speed processors, and unique bus architecture. The Compaq SystemPro, Mitac, and the IBM server series are examples of such machines. Another vendor, NetFrame, offers heavy-duty servers with extra fans, special channels to handle wiring, and especially large drive bays.

Hybrid servers are even more specialized. An example is an IBM-type server that is also a workstation multiplexor for access to IBM mainframe computers using a variant of the SNA protocols. In all likelihood, such a server will require use of the manufacturer's operating system.

Off-the-shelf high-speed microcomputers that offer the necessary processors and other features will minimally include a 40486 processor, and it would be wise to consider a Pentium or newer chip. Server hardware is regularly reviewed in *PC Magazine* and *LAN Magazine*. It is best to keep in mind that the server will need a high-capacity disk drive and room, probably, for three or four accessory boards.

A possible concern with server systems is the increase in cooperative development between hardware vendors and operating system vendors. Compaq, for instance, builds toward Novell software specifications. This may well lead to situations where only one operating system is available because it has been specifically adapted to a particular server. In such cases the vendor will be able to package the software with the machine. If the intent is to select a specialized machine, sufficient background work—including an online database search, vendor contact, and attendance at a trade show—is essential before selecting the server.

Server components may require more reliability than workstations, since servers usually operate continuously. Methods to insure reliable operation usually involve both hardware and the network operating system or other software. Consideration of the major approaches to reliability are detailed in Appendix D.

DISK DRIVES

Disk drives for LANs present ever more confusing options. There are drive sizes ranging from 100 megabytes to many gigabytes. There are fixed and removable media drives. There are magnetic, optical, and dye deposition drives. There are erasable drives, write-once-read many drives, and volatile drives. To make things even more complex, there are hybrid drive systems that combine a primary drive for immediate use with some other form of drive for long-term storage. For most libraries, an HSM (hierarchical storage management) system may not be necessary for the library catalog system, but it may be very useful for full-text delivery and archiving.

The most immediate choice to be made in selecting drives for a LAN is a size appropriate to the intended use. Generally one should select a magnetic drive with at least one gigabyte of storage. If your organization includes more than 15 people it would be wise to consider a drive with two gigabytes. This may seem like a lot of storage, especially since the first edition of this book recommended an 80-megabyte drive. The big difference in today's world is graphical operating systems such as Windows and OS/2. Along with graphical operating systems go graphics-intense applications software. Libraries have a lot more graphics software, particularly the software used with CD-ROMs, and even standard word processors use graphics interfaces. Storage requirements have therefore jumped from megabytes to gigabytes in size. The primary drive should also be magnetic, since data will be read, written, and erased frequently.

It is important for libraries and information centers to estimate file sizes that must be accommodated by the LAN. Specialized software such as library catalogs or retrieval systems will require a computation of file size based on the projected maximum number of records and the average record length. Other major applications software programs, such as a word processor or spreadsheet, ought to be dedicated at least 30 megabytes apiece. The LAN operating system will require space, probably at least 70 megabytes. The number of users also affects disk space requirements. Staff will probably require at least 10 megabytes each, while each patron may need 2 megabytes. A form for making an estimate is included in Appendix E. Finally, a CD-ROM drive is an essential component, not for routine data storage, but because copies of the network operating system are now distributed on CD.

WORKSTATIONS AND LAN INTERFACE CARDS

The world of workstations for LAN users is unusually diverse. Virtually any type of PC can be connected to a LAN, and there are workstations made exclusively for LAN use. Among the latter are so called "diskless" workstations that have no disk drives and are booted with software sent from the server.

The choice of a standard workstation is largely driven by the prospective users. To decide what workstation will best fit their requirements, you will need answers to some of the following questions:

- What is the primary task each user needs to accomplish? How many users consider this a primary or secondary task?

- Is the user going to make use of graphics software?
- How large is the largest file needed for user tasks?
- Will data be transferred from the LAN in paper form, by electronic mail, on diskette, or in a combination of these ways?
- What memory, monitor, and disk drive requirements are specified by the users' applications program?

Here are some factors to consider when purchasing new workstations:

- A hard disk in the user workstation will allow enough space for configuration information and a copy of the workstation operating system. Hard disks accommodate software that is either not LAN compatible or not LAN licensed. A fast hard disk is important because the hard disk provides temporary or "virtual" storage for large files when they are being read, sorted, or searched by the software.
- Floppy disk drives increase the possibility of virus infection. Diskless workstations require more initial setup effort. The value of diskless workstations is greatest in extremely high-security situations rarely encountered in libraries and information centers.
- The fastest, most powerful machine you can afford will remain usable longer than a machine that has already been manufactured for several years.
- Extra memory is particularly likely to extend the useful lifetime of a workstation.
- Color monitors with SVGA or higher resolution are a good investment. Users will find color important to them, and most software now requires such monitors.
- A pointing device is desirable. More and more applications programs include graphics. The current trend is to purchase a trackball rather than a mouse to conserve desktop space. Pointing devices should have very low force buttons that don't click.

To connect a microcomputer to a LAN requires an interface board that works with the topology and communication protocol selected for your LAN. The interface must also match the type of bus (whether ISA, EISA, MicroChannel, PCI, or SCSI) used in the computer. Choose a high-quality interface card from a manufacturer like 3COM or Intel, even if you are using clone computers. The gain in reliability and compatibility is well worth the investment.

Choose network interface cards (NICs) that are "combo cards" that support more than one interface. Such cards may have both thinwire and twisted-pair Ethernet connections, or they may have twisted-pair connections that can run at either 10 Mbps (megabytes per second) or 100 Mbps. Those that support thinwire and twisted-pair offer the flexibility of running bus-type wiring segments (thinwire), if you run short of hub ports (twisted-pair). The multi-speed combo cards allow you to start with a low-speed LAN and increase the speed as the number of tasks and sophisticated users grows. Of course the speed increase must also be met in hubs, routers, wiring, and other hardware.

Software to run the interface board is usually provided with the operating system, although some special programs may be provided by the manufacturer of the board. Certainly it is wise to obtain a diagnostic program from the manufacturer to determine when a board has failed.

Most LAN hardware manufacturers have a presence on the Internet, particularly on the World Wide Web. For this reason it is important for the LAN manager to have full Internet access. When new or unusual equipment must be installed, the ability to download new drivers from the manufacturer is a real time-saver. Similar access to some vendors is also obtainable via CompuServe.

PRINTER OPTIONS

One of the primary justifications for having a LAN is to share a high-quality printer. For this reason, printers used in LANs are generally top of the line. Most quality printers will print graphics as well as text in a variety of fonts. There are many features available, though, some of which bear discussion:

- *Postscript*: The original Apple laser printer had postscript capability. The program in such a printer enables it to print at least 35 fonts and to scale each font between 1 and 999 points. Usually each font can be rotated and printed as an outline, shadow, or italic. Other output languages, particularly PCL from Hewlett-Packard, are also desirable.
- *Multiple paper feed bins*: Users normally want to have both plain paper and letterhead available simultaneously. The productivity increase is usually well worth the added price.
- *Extra memory*: Laser printers will print lengthy graphics

only if they have sufficient memory. Extra memory in other types of printers helps minimize delay in moving data to print.

- *Optional form feed*: Many times it is desirable to print just one copy on special paper. It helps to have a manual feed option that does not require taking paper out of the standard feed bins.
- *Automatic mode sensing*: If you have a mixed inventory of, for example, Apples and IBM compatibles, you may want a laser printer that can identify which compatibility the data sent to it demand.
- *Ethernet capability*: Most LANs allow the printer to be plugged into the hub independently. If you are going to connect to Ethernet, particularly twisted-pair cable, the ability to plug into the hub means that the printer will be easier to set up, manage, and troubleshoot. Many printers that connect to the hub have the capability of notifying a designated user when paper or ink run out.

Whatever options are chosen for a printer, remember one important caveat: your users will become addicted to it. Users of a laser printer build formats that they rely on to convey an impression to people they do business with. After a very short period of time, they would prefer to do without you, their boss, or a reserved parking spot than to do without that printer. It will pay to have a backup printer either within your organization or in another department. Usually departments that are connected through an organization-wide LAN or a bridge will reciprocate in providing emergency printer support. You can set up a simple login protocol or redirection within the print queues to direct printing to the alternate site when your printer is out of service.

REMOTE PRINTING

Printers that are not attached to the LAN server are increasingly possible. Newer models of printers come with built-in LAN interfaces. A number of third-party vendors offer LAN interfaces that will equip any printer to operate as a workstation. These devices all allow the printer to be situated at any point in the LAN that accommodates a workstation attachment. Several approaches to printer siting are then possible. If users are clustered together in offices or labs, it is reasonable to place a high-quality printer in each cluster location. If users are spread out, it may be better to have a printer in a central location. In either case it may be wise to have a well-ventilated cabinet or closet to house each printer in order to provide a reasonable compromise between access and security.

GATEWAYS AND BRIDGES

Connectivity is the byword of networking. Once users are connected within their workgroup or department, they want some kind of outside connection. Originally modems were used, and it was easy to characterize access as "outbound" (where the connection is forged to connect between departments, or to remote branches of the same department, larger computer systems, or outside communication networks) or as "inbound" (for those users who have computers at home or portables they take to job sites). Connections that are transparent to users, such as those that are part of electronic mail systems, may still be provided by inbound and outbound modems or they may be provided by dedicated connections of their own.

To set up a bridge or gateway to another service usually requires either use of the server or the hub, or installation of a workstation that handles transmission of traffic with the other system. In some cases, such as when an inbound modem service is set up or when wide area network systems are used, a dedicated communication server system may be required for the bridge or gateway. Several typical situations follow, although you should be aware that there are many types of bridges and gateways.

An internal bridge between two systems occurs within the server. This is the case where there are departmental baseband LANs that communicate with each other over an intervening thickwire Ethernet or broadband system. The operating system normally is configured with software drivers for the local and interdepartmental LAN interface cards, and that is about all there is to it.

Hardware for connection between disparate systems may require that you dedicate a workstation to the task. In such a case, the workstation contains interface cards for the two systems and is considered a gateway. It is usually necessary to run a software emulation for the communication process that occurs. An emulation of the proper workstation protocol may be provided by a normal modem control program like ProComm, or it may require proprietary software to provide the protocol.

Two problems often occur in establishing a gateway. One problem is that to set up a connection, a "port" must be made available on the computer system to which you are connecting. This has technical, political, and economic ramifications. Technically, the interface on the other computer system may be software controlled. In many systems that means you must notify the system administrator and allow him or her lead time to give your interface an account, security clearance, or an electronic address. Politically, if the organization has few ports available you may have to wait for an available connection. Economically, the devices to which you connect on the other system are much more expensive than those used in the LAN, so you may be asked to help pay part of the cost. The other problem is that users of a gateway are likely to require a good deal more support because keyboard functions usually map differently between systems. A small training program and distribution of alternate keyboard templates usually is the minimum you will need to provide users.

To set up either a bridge or a gateway, the LAN manager and the operator of the connected system should consider the following:

- What transmission (signal) protocol is expected between the LAN and the other system?
- What wiring must be connected?
- What type of terminal emulation is expected by the remote system?
- Is a LAN-compatible version of the emulation software available?
- Is a port on the remote system available to establish the connection?
- What must be done in order to reestablish service when either the LAN or the remote system goes down?
- What security provisions are required to permit users access to the remote system?

If the bridge or gateway requires server-installed drivers, it is best to purchase the proper hardware when the server is purchased. Boards installed in the server usually require special setup.

UNINTERRUPTIBLE POWER SUPPLY AND BACKUP SYSTEMS

Before you can begin using your server you should provide an uninterruptible power supply and a data backup system. Each of these systems is inexpensive compared to the server; both are essential for operation of a LAN.

Power conditioning systems come in a wide variety of designs. It is not always easy to determine the characteristics you need.

An uninterruptible power supply (UPS) has the ability to provide power without delay, while systems that are described as "standby power systems" are primarily intended to support a system during a gradual brownout. The greatest risk is an abrupt power outage, causing any open data file to be lost. With a proper power supply, there is time for all files to be closed in an orderly manner and for the server to be closed down.

Automatic shutdown is a very desirable feature in LAN power supplies. Through a special cable and interface card, it allows the power supply unit to notify the server of a power outage. A program on the server can then notify users and initiate an orderly shutdown. Think how much peace of mind this feature might bring you when a novice crew is operating the circulation desk while you are away!

If at all possible, the server, hub, and any communications equipment should be in the same physical location, allowing all critical equipment to share the UPS. This feature is desirable in order to inform remote sites that the server is going down and to move crucial files to other locations for continued operation.

A recent innovation offers important power supply security for critical applications. An uninterruptible power supply card that is plugged into a workstation's internal bus slot will keep the workstation running during power outages. Workstations at the circulation desk or workstations that provide a crucial user service such as access to an important CD-ROM might benefit from a power supply card. The LAN manager should consider having a power supply card to accommodate an emergency transfer of files to another LAN if required.

Data backup is the other important component of the backup system. If data are lost, particularly data about customers or loaned items, your organization could suffer financially. You should be able to back up LAN data regularly, reliably, and quickly.

The key to adequate backup of LAN data is usually a streaming tape drive matched to the size of disk used in the server. In the past a lot of 60-megabyte data tape drives were used, but the technology has moved ahead to digital (DAT) tape drives using 4mm or 8mm video tape type cartridges that can handle at least four gigabytes of data. These new drives are more suitable for LAN use since servers today usually begin with at least a 1-gigabyte hard disk and rapidly upgrade to multi-gigabyte sizes.

When a backup tape drive is purchased, it is important to insure that software is also purchased that will adequately back up the LAN operating system. In most cases the tape drive manufacturer will provide such software, but compatibility with all operating systems, or even all versions of one operating system, is far from assured. If in doubt, contact the operating system manufacturer and also tap the experience of your local LAN user group.

Why is compatibility with the operating system so crucial? The reason is simply that some of the operating system files, usually called the bindery, must be backed up. These files contain information about the authorized users, the security levels for users, and the security levels for files. Even if all the data and program files were adequately backed up, you could be in real trouble if you had to restore the system from backup. Suppose your hard disk went bad. If you had to create all the security levels and user IDs from scratch, it could take you a week and you might never be sure you had returned the system to its original configuration.

At the very least you should consider backing up the bindery files to a diskette using the utility provided with the operating system. Having the bindery backed up on diskette and on tape will provide necessary insurance should you have to restore operation from the backup.

Two types of backup software exist, and their nature determines where the backup tape drive will be installed. Some less expensive backup tape software will only operate with workstation operating systems. These packages require the tape drive to be mounted on a workstation. More expensive backup software packages may be set up as netware loadable modules (NLMs) that run on the server. With NLM-based software, the tape drive can be mounted on the server, usually on the SCSI bus.

Be sure of your choice of backup system—you *will* have to restore your system from tape. LAN operating systems or servers change frequently enough that there is an excellent chance you will have to regenerate your system from tape about every two years. In that time, users will demand more disk space, hardware may fail, and the operating system will need an upgrade. A checklist for backup is provided in Appendix F. You should modify it to match completely the hardware and software that make up your backup system.

SECURITY

Physical security is the final step in preparing LAN hardware for use, but it is often overlooked until the first problem occurs. Consider the following precautions:

- All workstations and the server should either be anchored to the work surface with security bolts or be located two locked doors away from public corridors. Commercial security cables that attach to equipment with adhesive pads are practically worthless because they are easily pried loose with a screwdriver.
- Alternatives to commercial security systems are plastic-coated cables whose ends are swedged closed and connected to the workstation, or hidden bolts (with Allen-wrench heads) that connect through the bottom or rear of the workstation case.
- Workstations in high-visibility public areas should be equipped with security cables and padlocks.
- Areas where large numbers of computers are located, such as a lab, should be behind two locked doors when the library is closed.
- Windows accessible from the ground or a rooftop should have locks or closures that cannot be jimmied open from outside.
- Walls should extend above suspended ceilings so that thieves cannot come across the ceiling from an adjoining room.
- Personnel should be reminded of the need to check all windows and doors when closing up for the night.
- Staff should be aware that thieves often pose as repair persons.

Hardware will probably be less of a daily concern than a long-term planning issue once initial implementation is complete. Power and speed will be an issue each time a software package is upgraded. Long-range planning for evolutionary replacement of workstations is a desirable goal. In a small library it may be more realistic to consider total replacement once workstations reach an age where reliability is an issue. In some cases, older workstations may be used to support a gateway service, asynchronous server function, or print spooler where application software is not as dependent on memory or CPU speed.

ADDITIONAL RESOURCES

"A Backup Decision Guide." *PC Magazine* 8(December 26, 1989):192–193.

"Backing Up: Guide to Media Choices." *PC Magazine* 9(October 16, 1990):274–275.

"Born to Serve." *PC Magazine* 14(March 28, 1995):219–250. Discusses workgroup servers.

Derfler, Frank J. "Adapters: The State of Affairs." *PC Magazine* 13(October 11, 1994):314–315.

———— "Building Workgroup Solutions: 10BaseT LANS." *PC Magazine* 9(October 16, 1990):359–398. Provides classic information.

———— and M. Keith Thompson. "LAN Operating Systems: The Power Behind the Server." *PC Magazine* 9(May 29, 1990):109–148.

Henshall, John, and Sandy Shaw. *OSI Explained: End-to-End Computer Communications Standards*. New York: Wiley, 1988.

Jensen, Bert. "Souped-Up Servers." *PC Magazine* 14(November 21, 1995): 7–253.

Lipschutz, Robert P., et al. "The Versatile Network Operating System." *PC Magazine* 14(May 30, 1995):228–258. Includes benchmark tests.

Madron, Thomas W. *Local Area Networks: The Second Generation*. New York: Wiley, 1988.

Maxwell, Kimberly. "Building Workgroup Solutions: LAN Metering Software." *PC Magazine* 9(September 11, 1990):295–319.

"Network Hardware: LAN Buyers Guide Issue" *LAN Magazine* 10(October 15, 1995):9–66.

"Network Management." *Byte* 16(March 1991):154–219.

Siyan, Karanjit. *NetWare: The Professional Reference*. 3rd ed. Indianapolis: New Riders Publishing, 1994.

4 WIRING

TOPOLOGY

The first step in dealing with LAN wiring is to determine which topology best fits your organization and its geography. Topology is the pattern of wires that interconnect workstations and the server. The common topologies include ring, star, and bus. These and other topologies are illustrated in Appendix G.

The topology chosen must situate the server at a suitable site. In a ring configuration, the server is located along the perimeter and mixed in with workstations. In star and bus topologies, the server must be centrally located.

A vendor's product name does not necessarily indicate topology. The IBM token-ring system, for instance, is essentially a star configuration network even though electronically it is a ring.

Those who use and write about LANs have to watch vendor claims. One frequent claim is that ring networks are inherently more reliable. The problem with this notion is that any network can be made more reliable if the operating system provides error detection and if the protocol is capable of continued operation with a wiring fault. At this point, almost none of the prevalent combinations of software and protocol are fault tolerant. Most can be made fault tolerant by configuring a system with a hub. Choosing a hub is an increasingly complex task because of the variety of troubleshooting and management options as well as the need to match hub capacity to routers and any Internet, broadband, or other communication systems. Vendors and the parent institution may be useful sources of expertise.

Cabling must match the characteristics of the signal protocol used by interface cards in the server, the workstations, and the hub (if there is one). Every type of LAN (Ethernet, Arcnet, AppleTalk) uses a particular type of signaling protocol that operates at a specific frequency and type of modulation. Cabling must also match the topology. As an example, consider that token-passing network systems may be purchased that are ring, star, or bus topology. Each variation will demand a somewhat different type of cable, depending on whether the wires that connect a workstation are formed into one cord so that they connect back to a hub or by running from workstation to workstation.

Cabling for token ring is typically two-conductor wire bound into a single sheathing. Cable for thickwire Ethernet is similarly a two-conductor cable within a single sheath. Thinwire Ethernet and Arcnet use coax cable, which has one conductor as a solid wire core and another conductor in the form of a braided wire just inside the sheath. Twisted-pair wire is usually several conductors inside a sheath that looks much like telephone cabling.

There is also flat wiring. In recent years flat copper wiring has become available that can be installed beneath carpet tiles to convey LAN signals and electrical service. This precludes the need for wiring to run beneath the floor or through the ceiling. The added advantage of flat wiring is that the room layout may be modified without long delays or expense.

Obviously, the variable that will probably have the most effect on topology is the geographical layout of the organization. It is often necessary to choose a star or ring topology for work groups with some type of bus topology to provide a backbone to interconnect the work-group LANs.

SURVEY

The second task in dealing with LAN wiring is to conduct a cabling survey. Before the cabling survey begins, policy issues should be resolved. Users will want their terminals located in places most convenient to their daily activities. The LAN manager will want cable length kept to a minimum. A guideline is needed so that the LAN manager and users can negotiate. The basis for the guideline should be the maximum cable length specified in the manufacturer's manual for the workstation interface cards. The manual will also state the maximum number of workstations on each cable segment.

The wiring survey should be conducted by the LAN manager or the library director, along with a physical plant technician familiar with the building. The purposes of a wiring survey are

- to determine the total cable length required to serve all of the workstations connected to the LAN
- to locate obstacles that will require extra cable length, a specialized cable type, or holes to be bored in masonry;
- to help decide the best topology and location of the server

Appendix H provides a form for conducting a wiring survey.

Be prepared to note during the wiring survey where each workstation is to be placed. The total length of cable will be affected by the location of the workstation within the room. Other common-sense factors will apply here, including location of electrical outlets and the ergonomic arrangement of the office.

As the wiring survey is conducted, it is important to remember that LAN cabling is *signal* cable. Unlike electrical cabling, total cable length is crucial. Obstacles to signal cabling include electric motors and other sources of electrical interference.

DESIGN AND LAYOUT

LAN cabling routes should be direct. In offices where electrical wiring is run in the ceiling, with drops down the wall to each outlet, electricians will often apply the same pattern to a LAN. The LAN wiring should, however, go directly between offices or from offices to wiring hubs. To conserve wire length, it is important to minimize the number of vertical drops. There are many means to disguise wiring, including installing it behind baseboards or in surface mount channels located immediately above the baseboard.

Some open office areas present problems in bringing LAN or electrical wiring to the center of a room. Electrical service poles that stand between floor and ceiling are readily available and most models will also accommodate LAN wiring. Low-cost installation can be accomplished using PVC pipe for the same purpose.

Once the wiring survey is accomplished, start a file for the building diagrams, wiring layout, and work orders. You will need to consult them again for troubleshooting or when modifications to the wiring layout are needed.

The third task in LAN wiring is planning the layout of the wiring system. The topology, server location, hub location, maximum wiring length, and data from the cabling survey need to be synthesized. You may need to consult an experienced LAN user, consultant, or management information system (MIS) specialist. Be sure to ask enough questions about this person's experience to have some idea of his or her preferences and biases.

While the wiring survey should be a key ingredient in choosing a topology, other factors also apply. Obviously the parent organization's other data communications systems, the cost (or budget), other LAN installations, and the protocols that the library system software will work with are all factors. Be sure to document the wiring topology, assumptions made about where things will be located, and any special problems that must be investigated further.

PURCHASING

Toolkit. The next step in dealing with LAN wiring is obtaining the components of a cabling tool kit. At minimum you will need

- a crimping tool or other installation device (for each type of cable used) that fastens the connector to the wire
- needle-nose pliers, wire cutters, and wire strippers
- a volt-ohm meter for testing the integrity of the wiring
- a building blueprint or scale drawing

Optionally you may need

- an electric drill and drill bits
- a hammer and screwdrivers
- socket drivers
- a tape measure
- a knife and woodblock for stripping cable

Wiring. The next step is to obtain wiring supplies. Depending on the topology and signal protocol used, there may be a variety of special hardware items used with the cable. If possible look at an existing installation to be sure you understand what components are required and where they are located. Basic wiring supplies will include

- Enough wire to connect all the proposed locations for workstations. Since wire is acquired in reels, it is likely that you will have to order a sufficient quantity beyond what you need to account for contingencies.
- Specialized wiring such as Teflon-insulated cable to run near or inside heating and air-conditioning ducts.
- Enough connectors for all the cabling segments, plus a 15 percent overage. The extra connectors will cover those you damage during installation and those that test with opens (where the wiring is broken) and shorts (where the two wires touch each other).
- Lightning isolation connectors. A minimum of two will

isolate the server from the wiring if there is a lightning strike.
- Cable terminators to finish cable segments. Usually one per segment is required, but systems vary.
- Wiring hub caps for ports that are not in use.
- End-to-end connectors for cable segments that already have connectors and must be hooked together to extend the cabling.
- Plastic twist-ties to keep cabling tidy and out of danger.

You will have to choose the type of LAN outlets to place in each work area. Because signal wiring must have good integrity without strains, a length of cable long enough to reach the workstation is commonly brought out of a wall outlet. This type of installation is similar to the way many telephones are connected. Unlike telephones, however, most coax-wired LANs will not tolerate a user disconnecting a workstation; a disconnect can crash the system. If your LAN wiring system is like this, you may wish to investigate wall-mounted plugs with a "make-before-break" feature that keeps the LAN connected should a user disconnect a workstation.

INSTALLATION

Connectors used in LAN cabling must be installed securely and tested for continuity. Everyone installing cable should attend an initial demonstration of connector installation before the first cable is installed. Each person, whether library staff, MIS staff, or contractor, should be required to demonstrate an ability to install connectors and to test the finished product for continuity. This recommendation may seem extreme, but electricians have been known to install signal cabling with complete disregard for the outcome.

Cable installation may be done by a contractor, by physical-plant specialists, or by library staff. Cable installers can run wiring that is either out in the open or in a drop ceiling. Those who work in the ceiling should wear dust masks and gloves. If you've never asked whether those aging ceiling tiles contain asbestos, now is the time before you disturb them.

Out-in-the-open wiring (as in a lab) may seem easy, but there are some tricks. The wiring can easily be run along walls, but if you have workstations in the middle of a room you may have problems. The most elementary solution is to use rubber wiring conduits on the floor, or sections of PVC pipe between tabletops. More sophisticated solutions are available where large areas must be accommodated and wiring becomes complicated or expensive to run.

Infrared light transmission systems are available for use in large, open office areas. They are primarily designed for offices where "office landscaping" has been done with acoustic partitions. The transmission units are mounted atop the partitions and trained on a common spot on the ceiling. Signals bounce off the common spot, going from sender to receiver.

"Wireless" LANs are also available that send signals over a radio link. This wiring substitute is more expensive than wire. Stay tuned, because there is apprehension that a low-level radiation hazard will exist, particularly when dozens of workstations communicate by radio.

Special solutions are available for long distances where there is no ceiling, such as across an open lobby or between adjoining buildings. In these cases, the purpose is to connect just part of the wiring path, so one pair of transmitter/receiver units is needed. Two types of units are available: microwave and laser. Specification and installation are usually performed by the vendor. These systems may be expensive solutions, but they solve problems that could be quite expensive to solve with the only other alternatives available: long wiring runs with repeaters, or a buried conduit.

The final step in wiring is to connect the network to the server. Actually the server will not function in many LAN systems unless at least one user terminal and some minimum length of cable is attached. You may set up one terminal and a short length of cable in the same room with the server while you initially boot up. Probably the best technique, once the server is working, is to connect one segment of cable to the system at a time. This process may seem time consuming, but if there is a cabling fault it is better to have it found and resolved.

ADDITIONAL RESOURCES

Anderson, Rick, and Kevin Woods. "10Base-T Ethernet: The Second Wave." *Data Communications* 19(November 21, 1990):49–64.
Derfler, Frank J. "The Next Wave: LANs Without Wires." *PC Magazine* 9(May 29, 1990):295–318, .

Petrusco, Sam, and Vince Humes. "Hybrid Fiber/Copper LAN Meets School's 25-Year Networking Requirements." *T.H.E. Journal* 21(May 1994):86–90.

Rash, Wayne Jr. "Whose Enterprise Is It?" *Byte* 16(March 1991):107–112.

Rizzo, John, and Jon Zilber. "How I Learned to Stop Worrying and Love Connectivity: Networking the '90s." *MacUser* 7(January 1991):92–97.

5 APPLICATIONS

Computers are the most important new tool for enhancing productivity. Whether you are involved in manufacturing or a service industry or are self-employed, computers can provide information, control operations, and monitor quality at a relatively low cost.

L. William Seidman and Steven L. Skancke
Productivity: The American Advantage

To users, applications are the payoff for LAN installation. For the LAN consultant and manager, they may easily present the greatest dilemmas. Most often, users' expectations about the flexibility and value of a LAN collide with reality when they find that the LAN is likely to force them to standardize on a single word processor or that they have to buy new applications with multi-user licensing.

The way around this dilemma is fairly simple—communicate! Talk with users up front and find out what software they are addicted to. Provide them with site-license pricing and let them make the tradeoffs. Ask users to list other applications they would like available on the LAN and to develop a priority list of likely purchases (see Appendix B).

At the very minimum, most networks will need a word processor, spreadsheet software, and a database. Additional applications will be needed to provide connectivity between users and to support the LAN Manager.

As Figure 5-1 shows, applications software can be categorized by who it serves and how great a "reach" it provides. The wide variety of applications and the temptation to purchase every package that catches someone's fancy make a systematic approach to the process essential. The place to start is with licensing and purchasing.

LICENSING

Each manufacturer of applications software provides a unique choice in site licensing. The two most common types are a license for a few users—usually called a six-pack—and an "unlimited" license. An alternative scheme is to provide a basic license, not unlike the six-pack, and then to require add-on units for every six or twelve users. In the add-on schemes there may be software usage counters that must be "charged up" to allow the maxi-

---

Figure 5–1: Categorizing Applications Software

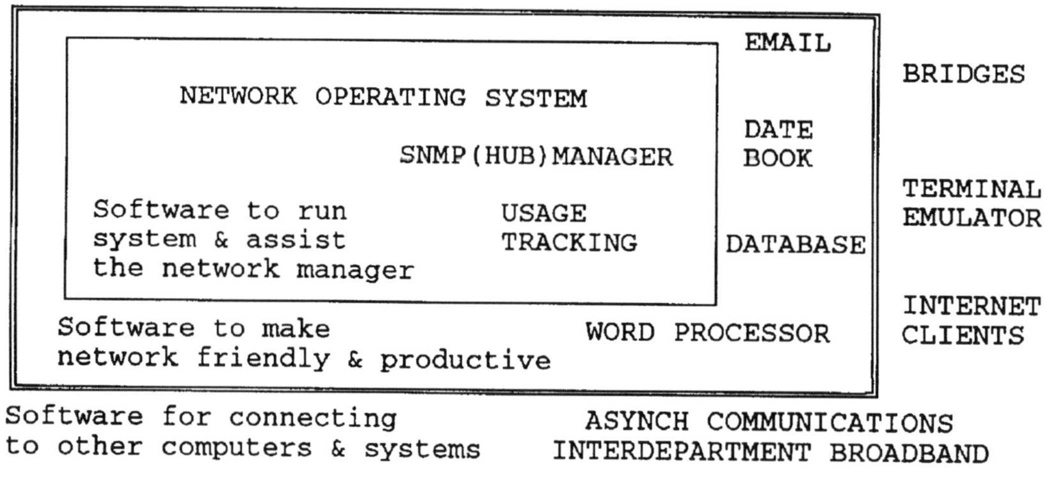

```
                                            EMAIL
                                                        BRIDGES
            NETWORK OPERATING SYSTEM
                                            DATE
                   SNMP(HUB)MANAGER         BOOK
                                                        TERMINAL
      Software to run           USAGE                   EMULATOR
      system & assist           TRACKING    DATABASE
      the network manager
                                                        INTERNET
      Software to make                  WORD PROCESSOR  CLIENTS
      network friendly & productive

Software for connecting            ASYNCH COMMUNICATIONS
to other computers & systems       INTERDEPARTMENT BROADBAND
```

mum number of licensees to operate the software simultaneously. A few manufacturers provide hardware locks that attach to I/O ports and prevent duplication. Most LAN managers will prefer to obtain the least restrictive license available. Small libraries can usually live with a six-pack, but the problems that arise when you upgrade either the server or the LAN operating system (necessitating backup and restoration of programs) make usage counters a nuisance. In many cases the copy protection schemes of some vendors make their products much less desirable.

SELECTION

Groupware. Network compatible software is often termed "groupware," and that may be a tip-off about how we should consider it. A LAN provides the perfect opportunity to connect users who normally work together on tasks. Most users want groupware to provide some fairly predictable things, such as:

- electronic mail (e-mail)
- shared databases
- standardized word processing (so that formats can be shared around the office)
- file transfer between workstations
- scheduling/calendaring

In choosing groupware, it is best to select individual software packages that each do one function very well. Initially users tend to want you to select integrated software in which all the programs use the same keystrokes for commands. At first glance this seems like a very attractive approach, but, when implemented, the results are often disappointing. The outcome is likely to be either that you buy a low-end package which users quickly outgrow or that you buy a high-end program (like Symphony) that only a few can master.

A good strategy is probably to select a menu system that will tie use of applications software into one system. Then you can add and delete options and customize individual workstation choices to each person's satisfaction. Menu systems are available with the LAN operating system, with current DOS versions, and with LAN utilities like the SABRE system. This obviously is not a problem in graphical operating systems such as Windows and OS/2.

What's Best. What constitutes a good application? Part of the answer is simply software that is widely accepted and whose features please reviewers. The rest of the answer involves some fairly important ingredients:

- screen drivers for common computer monitors including SuperVGA and any specialty monitors you use
- printer drivers for common printers, including Postscript, Epson, the Hewlett Packard Laserjet, and the printer you use
- a user interface that presents lists of commands so that you don't have to memorize them
- clear documentation that explains how to use each command
- cost
- LAN compatibility

Bear in mind when selecting software that programmers sometimes appreciate software for reasons that have nothing to do with why secretaries or desktop publishers would want them. If you are uncertain about a purchase, try out the software. Computer stores and user groups (both in person and electronically) can help with this. You should feel confident that your users will be able to use the software and eventually master it without also learning to hate it. At the same time, don't buy really simple software just because it's easy to use and often cheaper—users will soon outgrow it!

Standard Software. Standardization is the humbug of LAN managers. When a LAN is set up, it is natural to want only one word processor to be used, to have a single database software program, or to use only one interface for users. The best arguments for standardization are that a single software program is easier to support and troubleshoot. There are fewer problems converting between formats when you upgrade or change to another word processing package. Troubleshooting is less of a headache because the LAN manager probably does not have to be proficient in multiple software packages.

The arguments against standardization are that you constrain individual freedom and creativity and you may be viewed as a petty dictator. Users who have learned to write macros for Lotus 1-2-3 or forms for a word processor have a vested interest in continuing to use the software.

In the long run, it will probably be best to choose software based on its technical merits and acceptability to the majority of users. You may well find that you can't afford multiple packages, or that not every package is compatible with the workstation operating system you have selected.

Standardization has another side, which is simply that the parent organization may purchase a site license for a word processor, spreadsheet program, or database. Unless the software does not meet an essential library need, a site license can be cost effective—you are probably going to get a bargain. Site licenses may reduce price per user from $400 (retail) to $50 (site license).

Sources. Where should you buy software? The microcomputer marketplace is glitzy and the choices seem endless. Don't be afraid to purchase software by mail order. Once you own the software, support comes from the manufacturer, so don't be reluctant to order it from a vendor that is some distance from you. Care must be exercised in ordering the latest version and in getting the best site license available. It is well worth the effort to phone the manufacturer and to obtain specifications, product descriptions, and price lists. Good purchase specifications can prevent you from acquiring look-alike software that lacks the features you need. A few manufacturers will only sell through a local retailer, and most manufacturers will be able to tell you the store nearest you.

LIBRARY SYSTEMS

Library applications will probably comprise the meat and potatoes that your LAN serves up daily. You will want to compare what is currently available in the marketplace and choose the software that best meets your needs. There are several steps in this process, and it is wise to consult recent sources, including *Computers for Libraries*, *Library Hi-Tech*, and *Library Technology Reports*.

The first step is to select the software that will best meet your library's specific needs. Some of the major systems like Follett, Winnebago, Dynix, and Datatrek will have local representatives. You may well obtain a significant amount of information from vendor brochures, product demonstrations at library conferences, and from the literature. Do not neglect sources that provide critical evaluation of system operation. These sources include personal contacts, visits to sites where software is operational, and user groups at library conferences.

The second step in choosing a library system is to determine compatibility. The library system must be compatible with the LAN operating system. This is a thorny issue to take up with library vendors because they often supply their own dedicated LAN systems. It is important to determine the major LAN operating systems with which the vendor software is compatible, and to look into buying that operating system.

Most library software now uses graphical interfaces; this has particular ramifications for networking. In this environment, the user, whether library patron or staff member, no longer needs a handout or crib sheet listing commands—they all will appear on the screen. Functions are available that make it possible to track a book's status in great detail and users can perform many operations, including looking up their user status and checking out books, on their own. The impact of the increased functionality provided by such interfaces is that a more sophisticated workstation with large, high-resolution monitors, lots of memory, and a hard disk is required. There is a possible tradeoff—mainly that other facilities, including the user's office or a computer learning lab, can be used to provide workstation access.

An important consideration in choosing software is the relatively new notion of operational compatibility. Just as an open systems compatibility is required for hardware, it is also required for software. The most visible standard in this area is Z39.50 which requires sufficient client and server software compatibility to allow the user workstation software to access both the local online catalog and any other databases (such as other online catalogs or CD-ROMs) to which it is networked.

Another consideration for library software is the way in which client-server relationships are set up. Workstations can run client software that performs most of the tasks needed for some functions, such as circulation or cataloging. A few tasks, such as searching the online catalog, require fairly intensive work by the server to search databases too large to download to the workstation. The important aspect of client-server technology from a network standpoint, is to minimize the volume of information transmitted across the network, while insuring that as much processing as possible is done at the workstation. The extreme tradeoffs are that dumb terminals do not do local processing, and that more advanced database systems may download too much data—requiring a higher speed LAN to provide decent response times. Some further considerations for purchasing library systems are presented in Appendix I.

The next consideration is an important one: deciding upon a means of retrospective conversion. If you are compiling or using a MARC record database, one of the vendors or a regional bibliographic utility such as SOLINET or AMIGOS should be helpful. The data can be transmitted to you in either MicroLIF format, which is an abbreviated MARC record designed by the vendors for microcomputer systems, or in full MARC format.

After retrospective conversion comes barcoding the collection for circulation. This is a task with which many librarians are quite experienced. Use their experience. Try to barcode during "down time" when the library is closed. It can be done "on the fly" as patrons check out books, and that works well in certain settings. If you have so many patrons that they are likely to form lines when circulation is operating slowly, think seriously about barcoding over a holiday weekend.

One application that is often an alternative for creating an online catalog is retrieval software. You may decide to use a commercial thesaurus or to create your own, so that you can do your own subject indexing rather than relying on a MARC record database. If this alternative is appealing, the first problem is selecting software that will meet your needs.

Information storage and retrieval systems (ISARs) differ from database management systems (DBMSs) in the way that they index data. With a DBMS you can usually have the program create an index to a field (for instance, title) using the first dozen characters in the field. You are limited, however, to an access point that is literally the first word in the title, regardless of whether the word is an article, noun, or adverb. An ISAR, on the other hand, will index every word in the title field as an individual access point. Of course, a DBMS can be programmed to use every word as an access point, but an ISAR comes ready to go off the shelf. Information storage and retrieval systems even come in LAN-compatible versions. Some vendors may provide the best of both worlds. For example, SIRSI built an ISAR called BRS right into their sytem.

Anti-virus software is absolutely essential. Even if you have diskless workstations in public areas, staff will bring in data disks from other sites, software upgrades will come in, and bibliographic records will be transferred from other systems. Several capabilities are required:

- detection of viruses, both recent ones and those that may be several years old
- eradication of detected viruses
- reporting of viruses by name and type, preferably in a printed report
- workstation monitoring—so that each floppy disk that is inserted is automatically screened
- LAN compatibility

With new applications ordered, what is the next step? As each package arrives, it is important to back up the included diskettes. In most cases you will want to store the backups in a separate location from the originals, preferably where they can be kept under lock and key. The storage site should be secure; the theft of LAN software is particularly likely due to its relatively high cost.

If the LAN server is operational, software should be installed as soon as possible after it arrives. The temptation to wait for a convenient moment can be disastrous. The manufacturer's warranty will expire and free telephone support may only be available for the first three months. The countdown begins on the date of purchase. Pleading after six months that you just opened the shrink-wrap will mean nothing to a manufacturer who distributes millions of copies each year. After the free support runs out, most manufacturers will happily charge you premium dollars to call their technical support hotline.

TRAINING

Training for applications software is crucially important because that is what will occupy most of the LAN manager's time. In a library you may simply have to bite the bullet and rotate everyone through a training program somewhere, perhaps within the parent institution. Some shortcuts do exist however. The number one training shortcut is do-it-yourself. With new software it's often easy because the software comes with a tutorial. Videotapes and computer tutorials are available for major software packages as well. Just don't spend several hundred dollars to go to consultant workshops when you can get the same training with a $25 manual or a $60 videotape. A few seminars are worth the money, but they are the minority.

Training inevitably takes time away from the job, so it is important to do it well. If you have a choice, hands-on training is more effective. This can be accomplished by using a classroom equipped with computers or by running videotapes at individual workstations.

Computer literacy and computer phobia may be a problem with some staff members. Confronting this issue head-on can have unpleasant effects, perhaps even ruining an otherwise productive person's career. Two ingredients seem to work best in addressing the problem. One is firm positive pressure to use the computer. If each person works with some function that is automated, for example, the necessary pressure is being exerted. The second ingredient is an opportunity to be trained. Most people will surprise you. Often those who seem least likely will take off and get hooked on technology.

ADDITIONAL RESOURCES

Beaumont, Jane, and Joseph P. Cox. *Retrospective Conversion: A Practical Guide for Libraries*. Westport, Conn.: Meckler, 1989. Offers good coverage of the issues.

Breeding, Marshall. "Library Software: A Concise Guide to Current Commercial Products." *Library Software Review* 13(Winter 1994):280–294.

Costa, Betty, and Marie Costa. *A Micro Handbook for Small Libraries and Media Centers*. 3rd ed. Littleton, Colo.: Libraries Unlimited, 1991.

Dayall, Susan A. "No Easy Task? Training Your Staff to Use New Software." *Library Journal* (May 1, 1987): LC4–LC12. Presents a classic discussion about introducing new technology.

Kimberley, Robert. *Text Retrieval: A Directory of Software*. Brookfield, Vt.: Gower, 1990.

6 START UP

Getting all the ingredients together for a LAN requires a good deal of planning and careful specification of what to buy. Computers must be purchased, power and air conditioning environments must be established, and software has to be installed.

Purchasing, the first task, is tricky because you must purchase compatible ingredients. The people who do purchasing for your enterprise can be a great resource because they know the vendors in your area, the regulations you must follow, and the best ways to obtain discounts. They can't do the job alone, however—it takes communication.

You must communicate your needs and the decision-making flexibility that you require. If you turn all the decisions over to the purchasing office, they will then be free to make those little decisions, like choosing to buy multiple standalone versions rather than a network version simply because the standalones are available off-the-shelf locally. So what do you do to communicate well?

- Get to know purchasing regulations (computer equipment often requires special justification).
- Learn when bids are sent out and when they are due to return.
- Ask to review bids, routinely—before the bid is awarded.
- Find out if volume purchase contracts have been negotiated for the organization.
- Document what other hardware and software the item being purchased must be compatible with, especially the library system software if you will have one.
- Keep copies of all orders, justifications, and receiving reports.
- Install received items as promptly as possible to avoid warranty expiration.
- Follow up promptly on vendor delivery schedules and be willing to revoke orders once they go beyond a reasonable delay.

SITE PLANNING

Purchasing the LAN components should happen about the same time that you plan the site for the server. The site chosen may, indeed, have some impact on your choice of server. You will need a site that can house the server and the uninterruptible power supply for the server. The site must be plumbed for power outlets and cabling from the workstations. Also essential is air-conditioning that provides at least an "office" environment and airflow during the hours that the LAN server operates. Most servers operate without shutdown year round.

What constitutes a good site?

- The site should be located near the center of the area housing the workstations.
- Closets and workrooms that are locked after hours are good sites, provided that air-conditioning and wiring can be supplied.
- Desktop servers must be located on a solid support, like a counter, a steel server stand, or the floor. Free-standing tower servers can be placed on the floor, but attention must be paid to minimizing dust. Specialized racks and server tables can accommodate multiple servers.
- Space for storing perhaps 25 manuals, a large collection of diskettes, and a few tools must be near the server.
- Space for the LAN manager to use the server keyboard is essential.

Another decision to be made in site planning is the arrangement of printers. It used to be that centralized printers had to be attached to the server with a cable that could not exceed about 15 feet, and this is still a reliable way to manage. New interface devices are now available to attach a printer at any point in the LAN. Plan early to purchase such an interface if it is needed, because printed output will be an early demand. Locate printers where the staff has convenient and frequent access to them. Remember to choose a location that has storage space for paper and toner or ribbon cartridges. Wherever printers are located, you will need at least one letter tray or distribution bin for output that people haven't yet picked up. The tray should not be placed on top of the printer.

Not all sites will be conventional. Many larger organizations are able to position servers in a central location and distribute access over optical fiber backbones. Workstations are then plugged into hubs that feed into data switches and then into the backbone. Data tape backup systems are also often located centrally, perhaps in the MIS department. Departments share servers, too, provided they can find a way to share the cost of LAN management equitably.

TECHNICAL CONSIDERATIONS

What specifically is required for air-conditioning and power supplies?

- Power should be supplied from a circuit that supports no other equipment.
- Laser printers should be provided a separate power circuit from the one used by the server.
- Air-conditioning and heating systems should preclude subjecting the server to extreme swings in temperature. Closets are good because it is often easier to provide a small scale air-conditioning system. The server may operate for patron dial access even over vacations, so an air-conditioning system separate from the main system may be needed.
- Ideally uninterruptible power supplies should have a signal interface to the server that can tell the server to initiate a shutdown when power outages occur.

INSTALLATION

Every day is Christmas during startup for your LAN. New boxes arrive and you eagerly open and inspect each one. At the same time, you build a file of warranty information and send in the registration cards, keeping copies for your files. You spend some time with a tutorial provided by the LAN operating system manufacturer, attend a LAN manager training session, or work on an existing LAN under the supervision of another LAN manager. But where do you start assembling the LAN components?

There are five stages in assembling a LAN:

- hardware setup
- LAN operating system installation
- software setup
- workstation setup
- user setup

HARDWARE SETUP

The first stage, hardware setup, can begin as soon as you have seven ingredients. You need the server, the server LAN card, the uninterruptible power supply, the LAN operating system, one workstation, a workstation LAN card, and enough cable with proper connectors to attach the workstation to the server. (In some systems you may also need a wiring hub or concentrator.) Have your toolkit, manuals for all of the hardware and software involved, and a supply of formatted floppy disks at hand as well.

If at all possible, sit in on the installation of another LAN before you install yours. Otherwise, try to have an experienced LAN manager or consultant sit in on your installation. Even having a specialist available by phone can be helpful. The process of installing a LAN operating system has more steps and takes longer than almost any other software installation. You will probably do fine, but it is helpful to have someone who can confirm your judgments or clarify fuzzy instructions in the manuals.

Start by putting the server card into the server. You will have to check the hardware interface settings. These settings usually include DMA (direct memory access), IRQ (interrupt request line—a number assigned to each accessory that identifies the device when it converses with the CPU), and base memory, and they determine how the interface card will communicate with the server. You need to check the manufacturers' manuals for the computer, the monitor, and any accessory boards to determine the factory settings, particularly for interrupts—the IRQ settings. The network operating system manuals will guide you in configuring the server card so that it will not conflict with any other equipment. Occasionally you may come across another card, such as a monitor card or a memory card, that has extra parallel or serial interfaces that are not used but whose IRQ setting conflicts with the server card. In such cases it may be necessary to find out which jumper disconnects the extra interface and to remove the jumper.

Hardware setup should include wiring the premises and installing user workstations. In many cases the workstations are already operating and only require adaptation to the LAN. There are only three steps to connecting an operational workstation: installing the LAN interface card, connecting to the LAN cabling, and installing software drivers on the workstation. Installing interface cards, often labeled NICs (network interface cards), usually requires setting switches or moving jumpers as with the server interface card. MicroChannel cards are configured entirely by software commands. Software is provided from steps completed in the LAN operating system installation procedure.

OPERATING SYSTEM INSTALLATION

Choices need to be made and some information collected before the operating system can be installed. Information about the

DMA, IRQ, and base memory settings of the server board and any other network interface boards need to be at hand. You will need to know the model and capacity of the server hard disk(s) as well as information about printers connected to the server and the uninterruptible power supply. If you are using multiple hard disk drives, check to see if "disk mirroring" is available in the operating system and decide whether to use it. If you are installing onto a SCSI hard drive, do not try to reformat the hard disk during installation; typically that requires a utility not provided with the LAN operating system.

Read the installation manual to get an idea of the steps involved in the process. There will be steps for configuring the server, for configuring the workstation drivers, and for setting up any value-added processes (VAPs) or netware loadable modules (NLMs) that come with the operating system. Worksheets may be provided in the operating system manuals; they will provide you with a helpful outline for preparing to install the software.

Operating system installation can be time consuming, but there are means to shorten the process. One shortcut is to use LAN-ready hard disks that have already been quality checked (Novell certified) and are ready for installation. Quality checking the hard disk (Compsurf in Novell systems) can take hours. Another shortcut is to have the LAN operating system software already installed on a parent institution network to which the server can be connected, and to simply install over the connection. Another alternative may be to load the LAN operating system onto a workstation hard disk and run the configuration process there. The efficiency in using another server or workstation to configure the LAN operating system is simply that many more drivers and programs to support optional features are provided than one network will ever use. To configure the system from floppy disks can take hours longer because of the time you and the install program take swapping disks while searching for just the right driver or option.

More recent versions of Novell are installed from CD-ROMs. These versions require a CD-ROM drive in both the server and in a workstation used for initial setup. Installation is typically a two-part process. The first part is to set up the hard disk with a LAN partition and install a minimal LAN operating system there. The second part of the process is to install all of the operating system utilities from an attached workstation.

When the LAN operating system is installed on the server and the workstation software is set up, you are ready to log in for the first time. Usually the LAN manager is automatically provided with a Supervisor account that has security clearance to access any directory within the LAN. Once you log in there are several tasks waiting for you:

- Set up a system configuration file, much like CONFIG.SYS on a workstation. Consult the operating system manuals for advice.
- Set a password for the Supervisor.
- Establish a few initial user accounts and provide them with passwords.
- Make subdirectories for users' working files.
- Establish security rules for subdirectories on the server's hard disk(s).

The thorniest problem is usually how to subdivide the server's hard disk with directories. You will need areas for the users to store their data and an area for applications software. In most cases applications software must be installed on the primary disk (usually the SYS, or system disk) in the server. If you have multiple volumes (multiple logical disk drives) it is useful to set up user storage space on a volume other than the primary one so that users are less likely to have "accidents" that corrupt system or application software files. The following suggestions may help in setting up directories:

- Use subdirectories wherever possible to contain all files of one type or for one software package. Never install two software packages in the same subdirectory.
- Collect in one location files that users will want to access as a unit. Clip art, for instance, should all be collected in one set of related subdirectories.
- Acquaint users with the Tree command that will display the relationship of subdirectories graphically so users can see what's going on.
- Create a "home" directory for every user. Put all the home subdirectories under one general directory such as HOME—don't try to create intermediate subdirectories by user type. During logon a batch file should execute to change the directory (or to "map a drive") for the user to the home directory. Configuration information for each application should be set to use the home directory as the default location for files.

SOFTWARE SETUP

Applications software is installed on the server from a user workstation. This procedure is usually not very different from installing software on a single workstation. The most meaningful differences are the copy protection provisions, the location of software, and what mechanism is provided for user access. Copy protection comes in many forms and may require special subdirectories. The LAN manager will have to establish the subdirectories and provide security protection that allows users access without the ability to modify or delete files.

Normally, the LAN manager locates applications in subdirectories of the APPS directory on the system volume. With all applications located under the APPS directory, it is easy to set LAN security to protect that one directory and have its security precautions apply to all its subdirectories.

User access to applications should provide convenience and consistency. Users tend to like the security and convenience of menu systems such as those that come with Novell's operating system, or with Sabre or WordPerfect Office. These menus can be customized to link to the applications software your work group uses. One improvement is not to link the menu system directly to the applications. For example, if batch files are called from the menu and the batch files then call the applications, you gain considerable flexibility (see Figure 6-1). When you need to move a software package to some other directory, or when you want to insert a metering system command to track usage, the batch file can be modified without modifying menus or disturbing users.

WORKSTATION SETUP

Each workstation in the LAN must be set up with a network interface card (NIC) and the software to operate the NIC. As operating systems have developed, the software setup has become a bit more complex. There is usually one set of software that comes with the operating system and provides network drivers, and a supplementary set provided by the NIC manufacturer that allows the network drivers to work with that particular card. Additional components may be added to allow the workstation to use Windows in the network environment and to communicate with the Internet using TCP/IP. Using the most current drivers is particularly important for network reliability. In Novell NetWare, for instance, you might still purchase Version 3.12 which has ODI workstation drivers, but you are better advised to find the newer VLM drivers that come with Version 4. Trade tips with other LAN managers to keep up with what is best practice.

Setting up user workstation configurations is time-consuming, so it may help you to standardize the setup to make the installa-

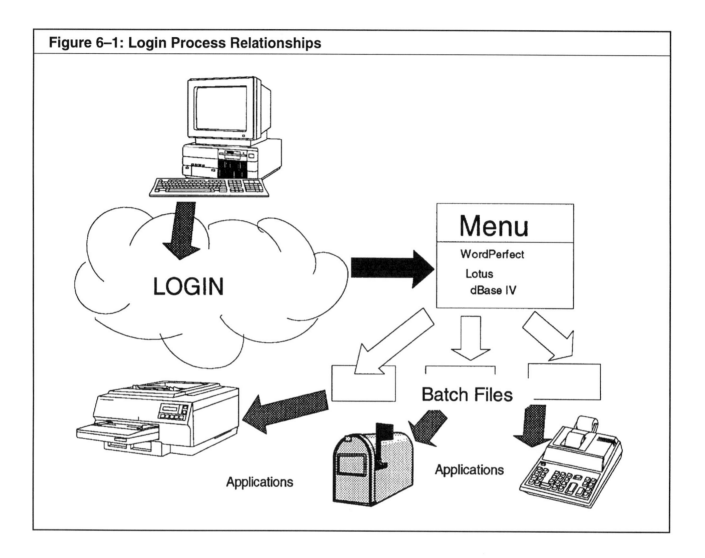

Figure 6–1: Login Process Relationships

tion process easy to replicate. Many LAN managers make up standard installation disks; setting up the user workstation can then be done by running an installation process from the floppy disk set. Another strategy is to load a typical configuration on the server, make each workstation minimally functional, and then download a full installation. Because the installation of the drivers often modifies complex configuration files, particularly in Windows, one LAN manager wrote a C-language program to copy the entire configuration of the workstation operating system and drivers onto new workstations.

USER SETUP

The final task in setting up the LAN is to help users prepare to use the LAN for their work. An initial training session may be feasible in some organizations, particularly in small close-knit work groups. Even with the best, most collegial training situation, there is some need for paper documentation of procedures. Initially this may be provided by issuing to all users an attractively printed notification that their user accounts have been established. Included in this notification can be elementary instructions for starting the workstation software and logging on. An example is provided in Appendix J.

The LAN operating system and most of the applications software will probably come with some command summary cards. Be sure to save a copy of each card in your files, but let the users have the rest of them. Now is a good time to provide a supply of keyboard templates too, so that users can have the smoothest transition possible.

While you are setting up the LAN you may notice an interesting thing—the LAN operating system, the workstation operating system, and one or more of the applications packages may have included games. Keep the games! If nothing else intrigues your users, the games might. They're great for tension breaks. And most important of all, they are one application that users don't need training to operate. Most games are fairly boring and will not compete for users' attention.

A cautionary note: when you set up the user accounts, give "supervisory" privileges to the LAN manager's and the library director's personal accounts. That way, if the LAN supervisor forgets a password, there is a way to reset it. When the LAN manager is on holiday, the director can reset user passwords. If the director is not too technically inclined, perhaps another LAN manager, someone in MIS, or another "power user" can be a responsible alternate to the LAN manager.

Does it all end there? Maybe. If your cable installation is clean, you are home free. Many installations may go through a period, though, where several connectors fail or intermittently act up. As you clean those up, it is typical to reach solid ground in a week or two. Occasionally there will be workstations at the extreme ends of the cabling system that misbehave or log on with difficulty; be aware of any such signs that might indicate that you have exceeded the specified cable length for the protocol.

Are you besieged by requests for user assistance? Even a small work group can take extra hours in the beginning. After five or six months, though, most users should be up to speed and they will be helping themselves and each other.

ADDITIONAL RESOURCES

Clark, Phillip M. "Developing a Decision Support System: The Software and Hardware Tools." *Library Administration & Management* 3(fall 1989):184–191.

Encyclopedia of Networking. San Francisco: Novell/Sybex, 1993.

Marks, Kenneth. "A Day in the Life of a LAN Administrator." *Computers in Libraries* 12(October 1992):29–31.

Rugg, Tom. "Installing a Low-Cost LAN—Fool Proof Tips from a Pro." *CD-ROM Professional* 6(September 1993):114, 116, 118.

Wright, Kieth. *Workstations and Local Area Networks for Librarians.* Chicago: American Library Association, 1990.

7 DAILY OPERATIONS

Does a LAN have a life of its own? The LAN itself doesn't require much intervention because the hardware and software are relatively reliable, but it requires some attention to keep it and its users functioning. Most of the attention spent on a LAN goes to support the people, software, and communication processes that operate on it. What will it take to provide the support that the LAN and its users require?

- support for the user's life cycle
- upgrade support for hardware and software
- disk space management
- system backup
- usage tracking
- system security
- print management
- communication with users
- training

All of these tasks require understanding the local area network, the workstation environment that users are tied to, and the applications software used in the library. While several of these tasks could be distributed to a number of people, you may be much better served if one person, probably a LAN manager, does all of them.

THE LAN MANAGER

Where do LAN managers come from? They may be drawn from existing staff, hired with specific qualifications as LAN manager, or provided as required from a central support staff in the MIS (management information system) department. There are advantages to each.

"Indigenous" LAN managers have real strengths in knowing the users and organization well. They can understand which users will need assistance with an application, anticipate when the organization is best able to afford upgrades, and find ways for the LAN to be helpful that an outsider might not appreciate. One problem faced by an indigenous LAN manager is that the organization often fails to recognize adequately the workload that a LAN imposes.

LAN management specialists may be either computer science majors or individuals from other backgrounds who have become certified. Novell training centers offer to credential people as CNEs (Certified Novell Engineers) and CNAs (Certified Novell Administrators). A minimum qualification is probably the CNA, and indigenous LAN managers can study on their own to become certified. Such specialists bring a theoretical understanding of the LAN, a broader perspective, and proven technical skills. The ideal technician has the ability to install, maintain, and troubleshoot a LAN. An added incentive to hiring a technician is the possibility that you are also hiring a programmer. In a small library setting you are not likely to keep a LAN manager busy full time, so his or her programming capabilities can also be put to good use. My own preference is for a LAN manager who is also a statistician, because a library often needs statistics that we might not otherwise think to collect. Whatever the background of your LAN manager, make plans in the beginning to foster his or her professional growth. Technical skills age rapidly, and continuing education is even more important for a LAN manager than for librarians.

Support from a centralized staff is great if people there are used to installing and maintaining the type of LAN you are bent on using. If you have an oddball LAN it is very likely that someone on your own staff (maybe you!) will have to maintain it. Support from central staff provides the advantage of good technical skills. The disadvantage of central support is that ultimately someone may decide to implement a charge-back system for the service.

Using a member of the library staff as a LAN manager does not present a problem if the person is a "power user." Such a person should be able to set up a microcomputer, including formatting the hard disk, and should be proficient in a word processor and a database program. Experience installing applications software and accessory cards in the computer is essential. What you want is not necessarily a computer science major, but rather someone who understands what is going on in the operating system, can tenaciously solve problems, and has the ability to describe problems clearly to vendors and repair personnel.

Librarians who are LAN managers must have proper job descriptions. It is unfair to hire someone as a librarian and then add LAN management duties without changing the job description. This keeps supervisory expectations in line with the work the person is actually doing. Be prepared to consider work on the LAN in the annual evaluation, in deciding about workload, and in a promotion review. Remember that this particular "additional duty" can be very demanding! A model job description is presented in Appendix K.

When do you hire a LAN manager? Try hard to have the LAN manager hired or chosen in time to be part of the installation team. This insures that someone from your team knows what options were chosen and why, what special settings were required to get hardware components to work together, and where specialized tools are kept that are needed to work on the server and the wiring.

HELPING USERS

With a LAN manager piloting the ship, the next problem is establishing a user life cycle. Activities in the life cycle of each user include

- account setup
- authorizing the user for applications, including e-mail
- providing quick-study support to users
- configuring the user's workstation
- upgrading the user workstation
- changing application authorizations as responsibility changes
- deleting the user account

As this list demonstrates, the user life cycle involves tasks that relate the user to the organization as well as to the LAN. A LAN manager must be "in the loop" and involved in the general life of the organization. You can't expect that to happen effectively from an office three floors away or if the LAN manager has great disdain for the users. In a LAN, as in any computing system, users come and go. In a smaller unit this may seem to be less of a problem, but it is important to realize that the user's relationship with the LAN requires prompt response and frequent access to the LAN manager. This is largely because a user's life is made much more vital and interesting by activities in the operating system and applications software life cycles.

UPGRADES

Software manufacturers seem to release significant new versions about every 18 months. Whether due to changing technology or diminishing profits, vendors will suggest that you just can't do without the added productivity. The most crucial software upgrade in a library LAN is most likely to be library software rather than something like the word processor. Be aware that in many cases you can postpone upgrades to the LAN operating system, the server hardware, and other applications. When you reach a need to upgrade the library software, however, you may occasionally have to upgrade everything else. Historic precedents are few, but it is not unusual in commercial software to see a software upgrade mandate a hardware upgrade. Newer versions of word processing packages have continuously pushed users to faster machines with more memory. Programs that use graphics or "wizards," that treat text as objects, or that have quick formatting features require faster processors, more memory, and faster disk drives. Similarly, the arrival of more capable networks has moved users away from workstations that had insufficient memory to handle both user applications and network drivers.

Users may experience the changes in operating system and applications software as major upheavals. When the operating system or the server is upgraded you have to back up the system and regenerate the server. The LAN manager will try very hard to avoid changing the user environment during an upgrade, but, if Murphy's Law works at all, one file or another will fail to make the transition onto a backup tape or back onto the server after upgrade. Once the transition is made, users will also need upgrade training, new keyboard templates, and new manuals.

The key to a smooth upgrade is a systematic approach. A checklist to aid the process your first time around appears in Appendix L. The checklist can be adapted to fit your local situation.

FILE MANAGEMENT

Managing the allocation of disk storage space can be one of the least glamorous tasks a LAN manager performs. Users gobble up storage space at a rapid clip once they realize that there is lots of it available. Most operating systems have some facility for restricting the maximum amount of space one person can use. Of course, there will be exceptions that you can handle with individually justified extensions of the maximum limit. Should you ask for a policy decision before setting limits? If your system will accommodate a comfortable limit of at least ten megabytes of storage per user, then perhaps it would be better to set a limit and worry about policy later. A wise manager will document the limit in user aids, on a LAN bulletin board, or in help screens.

A special kind of balancing is required when allocating LAN storage space for programs. It is very likely that, even if there is only one physical disk drive, there will be two logical volumes for storage. This allows the system manager to provide a reasonable division of space between software and users. Then when user space approaches the maximum allocated to it, there is a measurable limit that will alert the manager, without the space shortage affecting the operating system. In most systems one volume will be primary. It is very likely that the operating system programs, the bindery, and most applications software will have to be kept on that primary volume. This may require that you exert a bit of ingenuity when storing files. It is possible, for instance, to have WordPerfect software on the primary volume, while keeping the graphics files that go with WordPerfect in a directory on the other volume.

BACKUP

Backup of stored data is a task that must be done frequently enough to provide effective insurance to users. Most backup systems will accommodate both full backup of all files and incremental backup of just those files that have been created or edited since a cutoff date that you specify. It is good practice to do a full backup at least once a month, with "rolling backups" daily or at least weekly. Libraries where circulation and other transactions are recorded on the LAN should do a daily backup. Once every three months, a copy of your system backup should be stored off-site. A bank or a friend in another library may be able to provide storage for this copy.

Remember to document every full system backup that you do. Documentation should include

- a list of all the directories and subdirectories on the LAN hard disk(s) for all volumes (you may have to create subdirectories before you restore from backup)
- the date of the backup (so you can tell what's what later on)
- hard-copy listings of key batch files, printer macros, and typical user configurations (some things you can't afford to lose)

The backup checklist in Appendix F includes these items and can be modified to meet your specific needs.

USAGE

Tracking use of the LAN is something most managers will undertake just to document that the work they are doing is appreciated. In most cases the LAN operating system will provide at least a minimum record of use, usually showing the time period and user name. Analysis in a spreadsheet is a reasonably quick way to produce a graph, showing use statistics by user or by month, that can be submitted with the library's annual report. It is probably wise to dump statistics annually, if for no other reason than to clear the storage space occupied by the log file.

A more important reason for using some kind of tracking software is to keep up with licensing restrictions. Applications software usually has some kind of licensing restriction. It's terribly inconvenient, but you can allow use only by the number of people for which you paid licensing fees. A number of "LAN management" software systems are available. They will let you apply whatever restrictions are needed. Some applications allow only designated users. Others may allow any user to run the program provided that the number of simultaneous users does not exceed the number of licenses. Set up a program of this kind so that users are politely informed that the maximum number of licensed users has accessed the application and that the application is currently unavailable.

SECURITY

A LAN manager should review security annually to see what problems may have crept in. As each new applications program is added there may be times when security is removed or adjusted to permit adequate troubleshooting. The operating system will probably include a utility program that can detect inconsistencies in allocating access rights. Run the program and check to see that it makes sense. A good procedure is to annotate a printed copy of the security audit and keep it—so that you won't forget why you allowed certain exceptions. The security audit may also help get things working when you need to restore from tape. The annual security check is also a good time to clean out user accounts that are no longer current and to tidy up disk storage for projects that have been completed.

The LAN manager poses his or her own security problem and should have a personal LAN account in addition to the "Supervisor" account, in order to prevent accidental erasures. The Supervisor account has no security limitations; if it is used for word processing there is a chance of saving files in whatever directory the supervisor happens to be in. In addition, having a LAN manager personal account allows the generation of more realistic usage figures so that you know how much logged-in time is directed specifically to LAN manager duties. It's also not a bad idea to have the LAN manager experience applications software in the same environment as other users. Sometimes subtle security problems can hinder software operation and the LAN manager will notice them more easily in this case.

Another aspect of security that needs to be incorporated into an operational policy is the question of after-hours access. Many organizations simply will not permit employees to work after business hours. On the other hand, an important advantage of the LAN is the ability to connect people who operate on different daily schedules. Whatever the situation, the LAN needs physical protection after hours while reasonable access to printers is allowed for people who need output. The LAN operating system usually will let you limit the hours when each user can access the system. This will handle many of the unusual situations that arise.

SPOOLING

Proper support for print spooling requires that someone who routinely uses the LAN printer become very familiar with the process. Problems will occur when a user loads an out-of-date driver and resets a printer configuration or when a printer runs out of paper. Whether you use the spooling software that comes with the LAN operating system or other spooling software, hiccups will occur in the print process. The person you choose for this task will need to know several things:

- how to reset and restart the printer
- how to use "console" commands to check the status of printers attached to the server and the status of user print jobs

- how to load ribbons or toner and paper in each printer
- at what stock levels the printer supplies should be reordered
- whom to call for maintenance on printers
- how to kill print jobs and how to restart a spooled job
- how to send a console message to all users about printer status
- what the proper printer drivers are for each application program you use

USER SUPPORT

Computer literacy levels among users will have a good deal to do with how enjoyable life is for the LAN manager. Should the manager try to educate the less literate members of the staff? The litmus test for this decision is probably whether the individual staff members ask for help. It can't hurt to notify everyone that assistance is available, but consider a rule of thumb: Incentives to move novices up the learning curve are often best if they seem to be caused by a state of nature. The closest thing to a state of nature is probably a computer program that the novice must use to do his or her job—the library catalog or circulation system. There is a great intangible value in wanting to master something that appears to be intrinsically part of one's profession.

Do all users get their own software manuals? It would seem natural, but you may have a limited number of manuals. For instance, if you purchased software as a "six-pack" or if more people have been added as users, you quickly come up short. Rarely do we order extra copies of manuals, and it's hard to get them from some software vendors. Upgrades offer a direct way to overcome a shortage of manuals by allowing you to give novice or less frequent users the older manuals. Another approach is to purchase trade manuals and to give users a choice between those and the "official" manuals.

FILE SHARING

Probably one of the reasons you are installing a LAN is to provide file sharing between users. Planning is necessary for the LAN manager to set up and document for users the directory locations of shared files. In the library you may particularly want to have shared subdirectories for work groups or library functions. You might, for instance, have a shared directory for public services and another for technical services. You might have a shared subdirectory for acquisitions, another for serials, another for circulation, and another for cataloging. In this way all the correspondence, user handouts, and mailing lists for each function can be placed in a common area. In each shared directory it is important to set security permissions so that everyone properly concerned with the files can access them. By having access limited to staff groups, it is likely that you will automatically set up a good security barrier to prevent users of the online catalog via the LAN from accessing staff files. It never hurts to check for security. Some operating systems come with a utility program that looks for security lapses.

Another issue is files that are in the directory of an employee and whose supervisor needs access. More recently there have been organization-wide policies set for this kind of situation. In lieu of a policy, you might start by suggesting a shared directory. It is not unreasonable to allow a supervisor to have access rights to an employee's files, provided that the employee knows that this is the case. It is best for the LAN manager to take the time to explain early on that sensitive (i.e., personal) files should not be kept on the LAN.

COMMUNICATION

One application that users really need some familiarization with is e-mail. It is one of the most-wanted applications on a LAN, but it should not be assumed that it will be easy to learn. E-mail can be a lot like CB radio—everyone uses it, but few follow the rules. Most organizations can't afford to have LAN users zapping ill-composed messages down the wire or offending colleagues. The following is a quick list of do's and don'ts that you may want to paraphrase into some kind of document or online help for your users.

- Don't send messages to "everyone" (unless there's a flash flood on the way or you're handing out free one dollar bills).
- Don't yield to temptation—keep what you say within the bounds of what you would say eyeball-to-eyeball.
- Do compose your message with extra-wide margins, so all of the text is displayed when it's viewed within the window of the mail software.
- Do outline your points so that the reader doesn't have to struggle to find them.
- Do "quote" prior messages if you include them inside your electronic message, and give credit to the authors.

- Do make your paragraphs short and to the point.
- Do ask your LAN manager where to post electronic notices about babysitting jobs, cars for sale, and "hot" phone numbers.

How do you communicate with users? The obvious answer is electronically on the LAN. Some minimum paperwork is needed, though. The absolute minimum is something that documents login procedures, the new user's ID and password, and the procedure for changing passwords. A model for a new user notification letter is contained in Appendix J. Beyond this basic document, it is possible to rely mostly on help screens, menu systems, and news listings.

Some software for providing user bulletin boards or news listings may be provided as part of the operating system or a mail package, or it can be purchased specifically for the purpose. Something like Lotus Notes may be just the ticket. In lieu of a custom package, it is easy either to build a compiled BASIC program that displays news screens or to set up an inexpensive line editor that will allow users to scroll through a news listing.

Once you find suitable software to convey information to users it's important to keep it up to date. Notify users via e-mail whenever you update the news listing. Expand the news service to accommodate new services in the library.

The job of LAN management never ends. Most LAN managers, like MIS folk everywhere, get dragged into problems that users have with applications software, they have to plan for and cope with change, and they do a lot just to keep the organization running smoothly. The library has to learn to live with this new creature and the LAN manager who cares for it. Increased productivity and improved library service depend upon making the new LAN and the old library work together.

ADDITIONAL RESOURCES

Campbell, Becky J., and Mickey J. Applebaum. *Don't Panic! It's Only NetWare.* 2nd ed. Indianapolis: New Riders Publishing, 1995.

8 MAINTENANCE AND TROUBLESHOOTING

Technology allows librarians to be more professional, to concentrate upon the important, difficult tasks confronting them. Technology does not destroy jobs. It enhances and complicates existing jobs and creates new ones.

William Gray Potter
Library Software Review, March-April 1990

Some problems are going to crop up no matter how charmed a life you lead. Be prepared for those everyday emergencies. First and foremost, the staff should know what to do in a power brownout or blackout. Printed procedures alone won't help—staff have to know that the server must be shut down and power to it turned off. Shutdown usually involves giving a command to close all the open files and log users out. Typing one word in the dark is pretty tough unless the keyboard has "home" keys with bumps on the F and J keys. If not, you may want to do something to "enhance" those keys.

The next most important emergency drill is what to do when workstations freeze. Most personal computers can be expected to "lose a vector" or to go haywire in some way. The more software and hardware components there are in a workstation, the likelier it is that something will go wrong. Most heavy users will encounter a problem once a week. Word processors are a particular problem because critical documents can be lost to workstation failure. An ounce of prevention here is simply to turn on the word processor's automatic backup feature and insure that it operates frequently. Each user should know the name of the backup file and which directory to find it in when necessary.

SUPPORT

All of the remaining problems you encounter with a LAN are likely to be less harrowing if you have adequately established a support relationship with a technical agency. It is essential that there be someone in either the parent organization or in a maintenance vendor's shop that you can summon for quick response when the network server develops hiccups. A down server gives you very little room for maneuver, because, despite any disclaimer you make, users depend on the system.

What provisions should you make for support?

- Quick response is needed—usually within two hours.
- In-depth experience and technical knowledge should be provided because calls to a manufacturer's toll-free number are unlikely to provide the detailed on-site troubleshooting you need.
- Temporary replacement of defective components, up to and including the whole server, should be available. (Alternatively, you may be able to arrange support from another network server by temporarily installing a microcomputer with two interface cards to act as a bridge.)

A source of technical support is not enough by itself. You need to have a kit of materials for use by you and the technicians. Having the following items on hand will speed repairs and avoid unnecessary downtime:

- the wiring toolkit, including hand tools and spare parts
- a copy of the workstation operating system on floppy disk
- copies of the distribution disks of all your LAN software including the LAN operating system
- software manuals
- a spare workstation LAN card and, if you can afford it, a spare server LAN card
- diagnostic software for the workstation LAN interface cards
- configuration notes from initial installation and subsequent upgrades
- a scale drawing of the site showing wiring locations
- your problem-solving log showing recent problems and remedies applied

Get all of this gear together where you can lay hands on it quickly. Keep it in a file drawer or cabinet that you can lock to keep it from the depredations of people hanging office pictures or looking for floppy disks that aren't nailed down. Now, how frequently is this stuff going to be used?

PREVENTION

Preventive action is important—it can save wear and tear on your soul. Data about your hardware and software are particularly vital when there is a problem. You should have the warranty and maintenance history and other information available in an easily interpreted format. An example of a form that might be used to keep information instantly accessible is presented in Appendix M.

Routine support for microcomputers usually involves cleaning disk drives, cleaning mouse track balls, and checking to make sure airflow vents are open. A LAN manager should be aware of signs and symptoms that often foretell trouble—so that preventive measures can be taken. Thus, the LAN manager should also do the following:

- Take an annual inventory of workstations. Use the opportunity to check physical security, electrical safety, and cable routing.
- Be aware of unusual noises from hard disks and printers.
- Pay attention to heavily used systems that may develop intermittent problems with interface boards. Mild corrosion is often the cause and may be cured by removing the board and burnishing the contacts with a piece of bond paper.
- Wipe areas around monitors and air intakes with an antistatic cloth made for use around computers.
- Label LAN wiring. If two wires go to a workstation it should be clear which one connects to the server. Wiring hubs should be labeled to show which wire attaches to which workstation.
- Place labels on workstations asking users to call the LAN manager if the equipment needs to be moved.

Another form of prevention is to examine security procedures. Security procedures in the LAN can be one of the most direct causes of problems with applications software. As software is installed or upgraded, you may change security limits for some of the files the software needs to operate. Often it is necessary to protect the files for print drivers or the configuration files for a program to prevent accidental or malicious changes. In a word processor, for example, a printer driver must be set up, and users have to add it to their configurations. Otherwise, if the user changed the parallel port or fonts that the driver uses, that change might be saved in a central location and begin to affect everyone else using that driver. Initial configuration of driver set up should probably be done by the LAN manager. If there are drivers that need frequent reconfiguration, you may want to make a copy of the driver in a location where more specialized users can access it, and leave the original for everyone else.

RESPONSE

How do you respond to problems when they are reported?

One factor, that occurs before you even get a call, involves how rapidly and accurately problems are reported. Users try to fix things themselves. When nothing works they get desperate and frustrated, call the LAN manager, and expect someone to come help them quickly. A fair percentage of problems are caused by users themselves and are not maintenance problems. To minimize this kind of problem, the LAN manager must be free to provide help in a timely manner.

Another aspect of maintenance response is problem analysis. When a user reports a problem, find out exactly what the person was doing when the problem occurred. Note the software, type of workstation, workstation operating system version, error messages received, and any intuitive ideas the user supplies. Try some of these approaches:

- Follow leads suggested by error messages.
- See if the problem could have been caused by a security block or lack of familiarity with the software.
- Try the same operation on another LAN account.
- Run workstation diagnostics to be sure that the workstation is functioning.
- Check workstation, printer, and interface wires.
- Make sure that necessary paths, drives, and configuration files are available for the operation that was attempted.

As experience with the LAN operating system and applications software grows you will come to recognize some problems as soon as users begin to describe them. The key to analyzing unique or less frequent problems is to record enough information for you or a support specialist to work from. Keep a trouble log for the LAN as a whole and keep records for each workstation. A log will help you spot trends or related problems. Also note the solutions you find. That way you will have a record later that you set up a "work-around" or to remind you of the solution to some less frequent problem.

TYPICAL PROBLEMS

What are the most common problems that you might encounter in supporting a LAN?

WIRING

Wiring problems are common in new LANs. Most wiring problems come when a user accidentally strains a connection. A few are caused by faulty installation. The connector will look as though it is still fully connected, so it will take a systematic analysis to detect the fault. The most immediate response, which works once in a blue moon, is to determine if someone near a workstation might have nudged the wiring. Painters, phone repair people, dedicated house cleaners are your primary suspects. From that point on, it is a matter of unplugging portions of the wiring system to see if the fault can be isolated.

In LAN topologies where there is a hub, it is possible to detach terminals or branches one at a time until you detect the one that will allow the LAN to operate without it. In bus type LANs you will probably have to use the "ring of keys" approach—in other words you will probably have to open doors to get to almost every workstation with a LAN attachment. The actual procedure simply requires that you unplug one half of the LAN at a time to isolate the half with the fault. Next you re-connect one terminal at a time on the troublesome side, beginning with the one closest to the server. When you add one that brings the system down again you've located the culprit.

If you have a bus topology and you have a time domain reflectometer (TDR), now is a suitable time to use it. Initially, determine which half of the network has the problem, then attach the TDR at the head end (server end) and measure the distance that the signal goes. The distance should give you a rough idea of how far the offending cable end is from the server. Remember that when you have to estimate cable distance, you must account for cable running up inside walls, across ceilings, and over partitions as it goes to the workstations.

Once you detect the offending segment of cable, it is necessary to determine which end has the bad connector. If visual inspection does not reveal a discrepancy, it is time to pull out the volt-ohm meter (VOM) or continuity tester. If you are using a VOM, choose the ohm meter function. First test for a short by putting one test lead on each of the two main conductors at the same cable end. If the tester shows lights or the meter needle deflects, you have a short. If this test is negative at both ends, cap or short one cable end and test for continuity at the other end. The tester or meter ought to register. If it does not register then you may have an open connection. Once you detect the fault, it is necessary to decide which end connector is the problem. Probably the best way is to try slightly flexing the cable or connector components while the continuity meter is attached, to detect if part of the unit is loose and producing the problem. If a connector cannot be isolated, replace both connectors.

HARDWARE

What workstation hardware problems will you face?

Lack of workstation memory is a prime obstacle to the proper functioning of applications. This problem usually presents itself with very straightforward error messages. The most elementary solution is to get rid of terminate-and-stay-resident (TSR) programs. Hidden in memory may be small programs that are set up by your CONFIG.SYS or AUTOEXEC.BAT files, or by your LAN login procedures. Find out what they are. You can do this by inspecting the CONFIG.SYS, AUTOEXEC.BAT, and network batch files, and the LAN login script. A quick and easy diagnosis may be possible if you have a utility program listing the programs resident in memory. Two examples of programs that will give you needed detail are the Norton Utilities and the DOS command MEM. Most often you will find that there are programs that support a menu or that are nice to have but that you can do without. A little batch file magic can help you change the configuration files to match the LAN or the software you will use. There are even programs that will give you a menu of configurations and then automatically reboot your system in an appropriate setup. This can be particularly helpful if you use some real memory hogs like CD-ROM drivers.

When workstations are moved for maintenance or when you reconfigure their location, you may have to shut down the server to do so. In some systems, particularly thinwire Ethernet, you can get away with removing a workstation if you're careful. With thinwire you can detach the "T" connector at the back of the workstation, leaving the network connections intact. In many systems, if you are particularly fast, you can unplug a workstation and suffer only momentary interruptions. This is possible because most users are running software on their workstations, but not sending messages to the server. The LAN operating system will not usually be affected by a momentary break. Users who happen to be sending to the server are likely to get messages asking if they want to back up and retry or abort what they are doing. The downside of temporary lapses is that they can be terribly misleading. A user who gets an error may think the LAN is down. When you're not playing Russian Roulette with the wiring, a good professional worry for LAN managers is to wonder if your system is carrying the load well.

Server loading is likely to be a prime concern of the LAN manager. In a library where users are putting the system to good use, the server can bog down. When the server is consistently running at a 70 percent utilization rate or higher, it may be time to consider an upgrade. Related to server loading is the utilization of disk space. It is not uncommon for unchecked demand to outgrow disk space in a year. Once a week is probably about the right frequency to check utilization during a peak period when a full complement of users is logged in. This is probably a good time to eyeball the amount of available disk storage as well. Keep users apprised if you run short of disk space. A practical threshold to set your sights on may be about ten percent of available user storage. Don't count the disk volume where applications reside because it probably should not be used as auxiliary space for users. Of course you could maneuver software, graphics libraries, and other non-volatile files to make more space on the user volume.

SOFTWARE

The software drivers that make the network interface card (NIC) function are vulnerable to change in the workstation environment. When something goes wrong, there is a good possibility either that the workstation operating system cannot find the drivers or that parameters in the workstation environment have changed. Changes come about occasionally from user tinkering, but much more frequently from installation of new software or hardware. The basic troubleshooting procedure should include "remarking out" any TSRs, checking to see that the path to the drivers is still valid, then checking to be sure that the hardware interrupts, port assignments, and memory allocations are still valid and not duplicated by other hardware or software. Some of these determinations can only be made with troubleshooting software, like CheckIt, that can observe the settings. Similarly, in Windows or other GUI interfaces it is equally important to see that a LAN driver is being loaded and is not conflicting with other software.

Finally, it is a good idea to be aware of the possibility that either the LAN driver or some other software component needs upgrading in order to work with some other recently installed software.

VIRUSES

The newest problem LAN managers confront is the hazard of viruses. LANs are interconnected to other computer systems and users frequently import data to the LAN environment. Each time data move into the LAN there is a risk. Fortunately some effective countermeasures can be taken. First, there are virus detection programs written just for use on a LAN. You can screen newly imported data files and be certain that they are virus free. More extensive programs are available (such as SiteLock) that will check each disk that is used on an attached workstation.

An adequate response to the threat of viruses may include establishing a policy for employees to follow. (A model virus policy is provided in Appendix N.) Many people don't realize that viruses can come from "safe" sources, such as disks from the GPO depository program or software from a commercial vendor. A common-sense viewpoint is often expressed that the first time an organization has a virus infection it is probably a good thing because it heightens awareness. On the other hand, you do not want your LAN to become infected. LANs take virus infection poorly. A virus can ruin valuable files and infect every user workstation that logs in. The good news is that not too many viruses are smart enough to deal with LAN security, so far.

PUBLIC ACCESS

LAN service for public access systems such as library catalogs can be a thorny problem. In office environments, security rules permit users to access most software that is available. Library LANs mix conventional office users with patrons who access just the library catalog. The best approach is to permit a public access account to have rights to only one program or service. Setting up a few terminals for catalog access probably will involve some or all of the following:

- Catalog terminals need to log in without the user having a LAN account. You also probably don't want patrons to use the terminal for word processing. The solution is either to use diskless workstations or to have an AUTOEXEC batch file that logs the workstation in. (Use a DOS utility to hide the AUTOEXEC file so patrons can't edit it.)
- Establish the LAN accounts for the catalog terminals so

that those accounts can only be logged in from specific terminals. (In Novell LANs you can specify the identity number of the workstation interface card.)

- Set up batch files on the LAN to take the catalog terminals to a simple menu that includes the catalog, finding out who is logged in, news, help, and logoff. Write the batch file and menu so that if the user exits the menu system by pressing escape the account is logged out.

CONCLUSION

Maintenance and troubleshooting go on for the life of any technology. Minimizing the effort devoted to maintenance should be important just for economic reasons, not to mention to reduce our collective stress levels. Unfortunately some minimum costs will continue. At the very least the cost of system backups and support of a LAN manager will be necessary.

You will be delighted and surprised by the creativity that some users display in using the LAN. You may be equally awed by the dependence on the LAN that the organization develops. The best protection from overzealous budget cutters and LAN detractors is to not let the organization lose sight of the benefits. Know what percentage of the budget LAN maintenance takes. Know what resources it takes to keep the LAN going. Most important, know what results the LAN produces. Everything from better-looking letters to accurate circulation records and improved service may result from LAN activities. Projects are often completed that could only have been done on the LAN. Highlight LAN benefits in the library annual report and get credit for your forward-looking and astute use of technology.

ADDITIONAL RESOURCES

Dortch, Michael. *The ABC's of Local Area Networks*. San Francisco: Sybex, 1990.

Intner, Sheila S., and Jane A. Hannigan. *The Library Microcomputer Environment: Management Issues*. New York: Oryx, 1988.

Segal, Rick. *The LAN Desktop Guide to Troubleshooting*. Carmel, Ind.: SAMS, 1992.

9 ADVANCED CAPABILITIES

In my experience, designers and vendors of such systems are only too well aware of how completely their systems need to be re-thought in terms of a "networked information" rather than a "housed information" architecture. It is the buyers and funders of such systems who now need to recognize this fact and to account for it in their strategic plans and, even more important, in their depreciation schedules.

Paul Evans Peters
Computers in Libraries, 12(2):46, April 1992

Most librarians today can identify with Paul Evans Peters's words and realize that the information provided to patrons may come either from resources not owned by the library or from resources not located in the library. In the 1980s, LANs were well provisioned if they included off-the-shelf ingredients. With the basic three tools of a word processor, a spreadsheet, and a database program, along with library software, you had the ability to run the library and adapt to new needs. If the three general purpose tools could also be programmed using their own macro languages, you could really do some pretty good tricks. A budget analysis can be done in a spreadsheet and the results, including charts, transferred into a word processor for production of a report. A database can be used to select from address lists so that the data can be printed as address labels from the word processor. You could do a lot with the basic three tools, even supplement the library software, if you were motivated to read the manuals.

There are times, however, when the complexity of an organization or a specific problem demands more sophisticated facilities. Some possible problems and opportunities are discussed here as an introduction to further problem solving.

PROGRAMMING

Off-the-shelf software comes with limitations, and sometimes there are tasks for which no software is readily available. When users bump their heads on conventional program limitations, someone usually suggests having a programmer develop software to solve the problem. This is a good idea, provided that

- you do a literature search to be certain that there is no off-the-shelf solution

- you know who is going to pay the programmer
- someone is prepared to do a thorough systems analysis
- you choose an appropriate programming language that suits the problem
- everyone understands that a locally coded program is unlikely to have the look and feel of a commercial product

Why is a systems analysis needed and who should do it? Well, most of us would feel very uncomfortable if a programmer, hired at a fairly good salary, had to spend a great deal of time learning about library systems, library jargon, and figuring out how our manual paperwork systems operate. A library staff member, and a systems analyst from the MIS department (if one is available), should look at the task requirements and state them in a report that a programmer can use to build programs. The analysis should address the following:

- the nature of the problem that is being solved
- what data are to be input and how
- what quality control measures should be taken
- what reports and output are required for printing or display at a workstation
- what file formats are required
- who will use the system and how frequently
- security levels for access to the software
- life cycle of data in the system (how long it is to remain in the system and how it is to be disposed of or archived)

Even if the programmer has to supplement this systems analysis with some details and judgment, the time saving will be significant. Most of us will also insist on the library having direct supervision of the programmer.

What constitutes an appropriate programming language? Modern programmers can use the command language of a database management system like dBASE or RBase to generate new applications without having to develop a library of functions first. Compiling the program with Clipper or Quicksilver will improve execution speed. A productivity language and compiler, then, are used for basically the same reason that you use cake mixes as opposed to making the batter from scratch.

Are there tasks that call for someone in the library to write a program instead of hiring a programmer? A well-equipped LAN manager should be prepared to write a few small programs, perhaps in compiled BASIC, Pascal, or C. It's easy to develop a screen display of text to convey notices to users during login. A librarian may want simply to make a KWIC (keyword in context) index of some text. These are certainly tasks that are within the compass of the LAN manager or one of the library staff.

MAC VS. PC

Should the LAN combine MS-DOS computers and Macintoshes? This question comes up when there is someone on the staff who has become addicted to one particular type of computer or when there is a software program that seems to be optimum for some particular task but only runs on one species of machine. Having multiple types of workstations is not difficult, but living with the limitations may be a problem.

The combination of machine types can be made in either direction. It is possible to have an MS-DOS machine operate in an AppleTalk LAN and a Macintosh operate in an MS-DOS LAN. To set up either type usually means living within the protocols that will allow such connections. On the Macintosh-compatible LAN there is a choice between AppleTalk and TOPS as LAN systems. On the MS-DOS LAN the choice will probably include Ethernet or Arcnet protocols operating with Novell, 3-COM, or UNIX operating systems.

The biggest limitations have to do with file format, e-mail, and output to printers. Text files can usually be transferred between systems as ASCII files without any special codes. Graphics are actually the most easily transferred files because many of the standard graphics file formats can be used by many types of graphics software. The biggest handicap to data exchange is overcome with networking because users are no longer tied to floppy disk formats—the real barrier to compatibility.

A comprehensive solution to having both MAC and PC compatibilities is to have an Ethernet LAN with the Novell operating system. The operating system can treat the different workstations with pretty much the same level of service. Users will be able to share files and print to common printers.

Among all the problems that will intrigue you about the technical aspects of a LAN, none will have such intricacy or staying power as the social and organizational problems that may arise from people sharing printers, ports, files, etc. The primary necessary tools are the sensitivity to recognize problems and the enterprise to solve them.

SERVER SPECIALIZATION

Libraries within large organizations can easily become involved in turf disputes. LAN and MIS managers do not want competition for users or for services. Centralization can be sold to management as a means to keep technical personnel resources (programmers and LAN managers) from proliferating in user departments. So just why does the library have to have its own LAN?

The best answer is that the library will use specialized software to access a relatively large database. Circulation and acquisitions represent a specialized set of transaction processing systems that demand a knowledge of library practice to set up and operate.

Within the larger organization it is not uncommon to find LANs specialized by function. This works to the library's advantage in that the services provided by the library, particularly catalog access and current awareness, can be provided over the LAN to users attached through their own departmental LANs. Specialization also favors the library if other servers already have word processing, database, spreadsheet, and other applications for which a site license has been obtained. If the site license extends throughout the larger organization, the library staff can obtain access to the appropriate LANs, minimizing the number of applications that must be installed on the library server and perhaps reducing software costs significantly.

Naturally, there are some risks to having specialized servers. One risk is the obvious likelihood that some servers may be down at unexpected times. Another risk is that different departments may not be able to accommodate each other's use of disk storage. Finally, there is the possibility that some of the cooperating departments will face problems funding their server and will attempt cost recovery from other departments.

The advantages of specialization can usually be shown to outweigh the disadvantages. If the cooperating departments are geographically compact enough, they can occupy a single LAN segment without having to connect through a broadband or other intervening LAN. LAN management overhead may be reduced by having one manager supporting all the specialized servers. Duplication can cover equipment failures. When a cooperating server goes down, backup tapes can be used to restore critical functions on another server, and service can be restored faster than maintenance personnel can replace the problem server.

OTHER EFFECTS

Another organizationally related problem is the impact that implementing a LAN will have on the people in the library. We hope for some direct productivity increases, better products and services, and improved coordination between people. Unexpected effects include new interpersonal relationships and tools for mischief as well as work.

Interpersonal relationships in an organization often revolve around the coffee pot and mail room. When you implement e-mail you begin to decrease the interaction that people are used to. There are two consequences—people will develop stronger ties with their closest workmates and they may feel more confined to their work area. Be sure that you allow people to take breaks in common areas that cut across organizational boundaries. It is also important that people take ergonomic breaks. When you work at a computer screen for an hour or two, it is necessary to go outside or to a window to let your eye muscles relax. Fix your gaze on some object that is about a mile away so that the muscles around your iris can relax. Standing up and moving around helps other muscles as well.

Electronic interactions also require some electronic etiquette. With e-mail you gain the benefit of being able to keep "receipts" that show when a message containing appointments, commitments, or deadlines was sent. You also lose the ability to make excuses because other people have their receipts.

Mischief can occur in a LAN environment as it can anywhere else. A smart user can certainly find a way to manipulate a batch file or some other weak link in your security net to play pranks on other users. At its worst, a poorly supervised LAN might allow a user to spy on other people's work or to tinker with their data. E-mail adds an unobtrusive way for people to "hit" on each other for dates and personal favors. None of us wants to play policeman or to have ugly situations develop, so the best solution is prevention. Have tight security on the LAN and coach users about LAN etiquette. Suspend a user's account if that person becomes really obnoxious. Be sure to document suspensions so that your library director knows what is going on. If suspension is impractical due to the nature of work that someone does, you may have no recourse but to pursue bad conduct as a disciplinary problem.

VIRTUAL LIBRARIES

Creative and exciting possibilities exist for library LANs. Exploration of the ways that the LAN can be used to provide new services have only begun. One significant creative possibility is the notion of a virtual library.

The virtual library is a synthesizing concept for LAN development. It consists of resources that are "virtually" in the library. Online databases, full-text CD-ROM databases, LAN-based databases, and LAN-based CD-ROMs are all possible ingredients in establishing this kind of environment in your library. The virtual library concept tends to encompass nontraditional technologically accessed materials (such as videodisc) because they compress data into very compact forms of storage. A LAN is an important ingredient in making the virtual library possible.

When the library works within a networked environment, materials can be acquired, accessed, requested, and delivered—all electronically. Both users and materials can be located outside the four walls of the library. Beyond concerns about access and delivery, the virtual library offers a unique opportunity to increase library visibility and effectiveness.

When the library catalog, in-house databases, CD-ROMs, and reference service are made available through an enterprise-wide network, perceptions change. The library's value to the organization can increase significantly because we are bringing information to the user's desktop as envisioned in the notion of Memex proposed by Vannevar Bush in 1945.[1] Reaching the desktop is crucial because, as Victor Rosenberg pointed out in 1967, users do not want to travel far to obtain materials.[2] Many libraries already predicate their operations on this assumption; they locate in the geographic center of their territory and offer delivery service. The really important ingredient in the virtual library is remembering that service must always strive to reach out to the patron.

While some services like CD-ROMs may seem very obvious, what kind of creative activities does a LAN make possible? Following are some "crazy ideas" that might spur you to think of some more:

- If patrons have to go from one part of the library or from one branch to another, forward a physical description of the patron in an e-mail message telling a colleague that the patron is being referred. This way the patron will be recognized at the other end, which will win some points for the library.

- Have a programmer or power user write a macro that will walk someone through completion of an inter-library loan request form. Library patrons in other departments can run the program and e-mail the resulting file right to the staff member who does inter-library loan.

- Ask the programmer to write a macro that will take output from record in a frequently used database and format it into the inter-library loan form.

- Set up some tutorials, text databases, and maybe an organizational database on your server for patrons to access from their own department.

- Use a notebook or database program to keep a calendar of library activities, appointments, and deadlines.

- Put the budget, with "read only" security, where everyone on the staff can refer to it.

- Compile a list of article titles from the table of contents of one or two journals that everyone in the organization needs to read. Route the information via e-mail to everyone who wants it. They can send an e-mail response if they want you to send them a copy of an article.

- Provide access to informative Internet resources such as a gopher at a state or federal agency, the catalogs of other institutions in the local area, or a newsgroup of interest to patrons.

- Link all of the above suggestions to a common menu for use by staff members.

- If the Library is using Windows and also has Internet access, World Wide Web resources may be linked to bookmarks in the browser or set up on a Web server for library patrons to access from home.

LAN use in your library may be strictly utilitarian, free wheeling, or aggressively entrepreneurial. Regardless of the pattern, you will need to consider carefully the impact LAN technology will have on the organization.

ADDITIONAL RESOURCES

Cain, Mark. "Simple and Inexpensive CD-ROM Networking: A Step-by-Step Approach." *Information Technology and Libraries* 12(June 1993):262–266.

Daly, Kevin F. "A Planning Guide for Instructional Networks" *Computer Teacher* 22(September 1994):11–12, 14–15.

Eager, William. "Benefits and Challenges of Distributing Multimedia over Local and Wide Area Networks." *Journal of Instruction Delivery Systems* 7(winter 1993):11–14.

"Electronic School." *Executive Educator* 16(September 1994):A1–A56.

Marks, Kenneth E. "LANS: A Moving Experience." *Computers in Libraries* 13(April 1993):19–21.

Starr, Karen J. "NetWare Loadable Modules for CD-ROM Networking." *CD-ROM Professional* 6(November 1993):82, 84–87.

ENDNOTES

1. Bush, Vannevar. "As We May Think." *Atlantic Monthly* 176(July 1945):101–108.

2. Rosenberg, Victor. "Factors Affecting the Preferences of Industrial Personnel for Information Gathering Methods." *Information Storage and Retrieval* 3(July 1967)

10 CONNECTIONS

The ability of libraries to engage in two-way, multimedia communication not only with other libraries but with their own users is likely to bring about an important change in the role of the library as a social institution. By devising means for direct use of materials, the library community will have created an educational and research capability more versatile than anything previously developed.

Robert M. Hayes
Joseph Becker
Handbook of Data Processing for Libraries

Electronic systems have opened a new dimension for libraries as a communication environment where users can have information delivered to them electronically. A library that installs a LAN will be better able to meet the barrage of requests for new electronically delivered services.

Libraries face tremendous growth in delivery of electronic services over the next few years. Librarians have been key players in supporting national networking through the National Research and Education Network (NREN), the National Information Infrastructure (NII), and other federal programs that have sought congressional support. Delivery of electronic access services such as remote use of OPACs at public libraries is a reality in many places. Electronic publishing is another source of growth, particularly through full-text databases and via the World Wide Web. Project Gutenberg, projects supported by OCLC, and CARL provide on-demand distribution of electronic texts. Publishers are finding new ways of packaging electronic texts in hypertext software and in convenient CD-ROM sets. Many libraries now routinely use the Internet and the World Wide Web for internal functions (such as reference, cataloging, and collection development) and as an additional resource for patrons. The net result is further demand by library patrons for electronic documents and connectivity.

Connectivity is at present a relatively complex activity and the effort expended to improve it has to be matched by real benefits. Each link outside the local LAN server usually requires unique software and possibly additional hardware. Each connection may also require administration of user passwords, configuration support for users, and training. Ideally the training component should be less a matter of formal training and more a matter of providing good on-screen helps and good handouts for users.

Most services that the library might connect with are likely to involve a bridge, gateway, router, modem, or specialized server.

Some kind of black-box connection has to be used to route the user to the service and translate signals so that the user can work with the service. A number of devices are needed to set up a connection.

- Bridges establish a pathway to another computer system where the commands and security do not differ markedly from the user's own LAN environment. In a microcomputer server, a bridge may be established by installing a second LAN card and installing appropriate software. If the protocol is not different, the connection may simply be made through the LAN hub or via a broadband system to which the LAN is connected.
- Gateways typically establish connections to systems where the command protocols and security features are quite different. The hardware to set up a gateway may be as simple as an accessory card or may require specialized communication boxes.
- Routers are one species of specialized communication gear used in gateways. The router usually connects networks that differ in size, however, and it usually has the ability to detect messages destined for its local clients.
- Modems and facsimile equipment can be used to bring public telephone system connections into reach of LAN users. A variety of options make installation of a card in the server sufficient to provide service.
- CD-ROM servers are specialized LAN units that allow multiple users access a single database. Such systems are very expensive and are suitable for distributing access within the library and within the larger organization.

Each of these systems will demand time from the LAN manager. Time is needed to specify, acquire, configure, and install the equipment. Each adds an element of complexity to befuddle users, so time must be spent training users and solving user problems. Four steps can simplify the process of establishing new systems:

- Install new interfaces after the LAN has been up and running for a while—so that users are accustomed to the system and technical problems have settled down.
- Try out the new communication process. Be sure that your most naive user can understand how to operate it.
- Embed access to the process in a user menu or graphical user interface (GUI) and minimize the actions the user must take to initialize the software.

- Let everyone know that you are ready to help them with problems.

Three of these systems—the bridges, gateways, and routers—are best selected with the assistance of the MIS department or a LAN specialty vendor who is familiar with the options.

ASYNCHRONOUS COMMUNICATIONS

Most users would like to have remote access to the numerous databases that are available in the library—the library catalog and the CD-ROMs, for example. The key ingredient in providing access is to set up asynchronous communications between the LAN and the public telephone system. Two techniques are available: using an asynchronous LAN server or setting up a system for SLIP/PPP access, probably with a UNIX system as the primary host.

The first method to accomplish telephone access through the LAN is to install an asynchronous server card in the LAN server. Such cards typically have the capacity to manage up to six connections to modems tied into telephone lines. Each channel on the card has a CPU chip that acts just like a workstation to run the communication software and manage data transfer. Software is likely to be either a common modem control program or a program that is tailored to operate with the asynchronous server.

The second possibility for asynchronous communications is to set up the SLIP/PPP access. This is typically done with Windows or Macintosh client software which dials a UNIX host system for services. The system operates TCP/IP protocol and is able to deliver Internet access to the extent that is desirable. In some locations the library is part of a group of community organizations that provide "freenet" service so that people in the community can have Internet access. In larger cities there are likely to be commercial providers who can deliver such services. With the capabilities that SLIP/PPP access provides, library patrons may be able to access the online catalog, CD-ROMs, and Internet resources.

A special benefit to having an asynchronous communications capability is that it provides both dial-out and dial-in capabilities. This capability would allow you to set up a port for users to dial in to the library catalog. It can also assist the LAN manager in handling problems from home on nights and weekends. Staff may find it very useful to access the LAN from home, especially when they are ill and cannot come in. Staff can use the common bank of modems to call out to DIALOG, and patrons can call in to use CD-ROM databases.

To set up a dial-in capability, it is particularly useful to have multiple phone lines (all responding to a single telephone number) for the modems. A phone bank like this (called a rotary) allows the library to publicize a single phone number and thereby improve user convenience.

When establishing an asynchronous system it is important that you do the following:

- Obtain the highest baud rate modem capability that will operate with the software operating them. Most modems will auto-detect the baud rate of the calling modem.
- If the asynchronous server is a server card, specify your server's bus interface (ISA, EISA, SCSI, or microchannel).
- Insure that asynchronous software is network capable.

Administratively, the asynchronous access system will require some care in establishing security measures. For staff access, a call-back system in the software provides a good degree of protection if you can check the phone number of the calling party against an authorization list. You also need to decide who, if anyone, will be allowed to upload to your LAN server from a remote location and whether external users will be allowed to exit the modem control program to the DOS prompt. One possible solution is to use personal LAN accounts with specific permissions for staff users and a highly restricted general purpose account for all other users.

CD-ROM ACCESS

An important means of bringing databases into the LAN is through a CD-ROM server. Such a server provides several CD-ROM drives and is tied in to the LAN in much the same way that workstations are wired in. The operation of a CD-ROM server is a complicated business initially. A variety of factors make CDs complex.

- Users may have to configure their workstations with extra drivers for the CDs, usually involving the Microsoft extensions for disk access.

- Not all CD-ROMs have the same software interface. Users may have to learn several command systems unless you are able to stay within one vendor's product line.
- Most of the interface programs are memory hogs and many CD-ROMs will not run on a LAN.

There are three types of LAN access for CD-ROMs: redirectors, where the software to access the CD-ROM is moved to the user's workstation on demand; NLM-based systems, where the software to access the CD-ROM runs on the server; and peer access, where CD-ROMs are installed on user workstations and shared between users. Peer access is probably not an acceptable solution in a library environment, but both redirector and NLM systems are server-based and will work. When purchasing CD-ROM servers it is important to realize that there are many vendors, but only a few actually build the systems. Four vendors seem to be the best known: Meridian, CBIS, Online Systems, and Micro Design International.

INTERNET CONNECTIONS

Adding an Internet connection is an additional step that can really expand the services provided by the library. Particularly with World Wide Web access, the library can be author, service provider, and organizational facilitator if it is willing. At a minimum, access may be provided only for e-mail access, but most libraries will want to connect a Web client that runs in a Windows or Macintosh desktop environment with full multimedia output. Two types of access are possible. A minimal mode of access is for the library to have dial-up modem access to the Internet service provider. Using fast modems makes this a viable option, but use by multiple users is unlikely and response time will be affected. A robust Internet connection will be made over a dedicated phone line that allows higher data transfer speeds and a noise-free connection. Communication equipment costs and monthly costs for a dedicated line are at least an order of magnitude greater.

Some libraries will want to have their own Web server. This is an increasingly easy system to establish, with software that can run on a Windows/Intel, a UNIX/Intel, or Macintosh platform. The primary concern is the availability of a suitably talented staff member to set up and maintain the additional server. Fortunately the overhead for such a system is not as great as for the LAN server, because there are no user accounts or user infrastructure to maintain.

The scope of Internet access is a concern in many libraries, where providing external dial-up access should not compete with commercial access providers, and where restricting the scope of accessible materials may be necessary for children. Such concerns may be readily addressed with software and security controls, still leaving the library free to be an important component in authoring local Web information products. The library may choose to make serials lists, current awareness materials, library hours, and library policies accessible on the library's or the parent institution's Web server.

OTHER TECHNOLOGIES

One communication product that you can set up in many LANs is a software interconnection to minicomputers or other systems that are made part of the LAN environment across a broadband connection. For instance, the library might be connected to an administrative computer running the UNIX operating system, in order to provide access to administrative services or to authoring space for Web homepages. Both a hardware interface and appropriate software are required for such a connection. These systems typically are Ethernet systems, operating over CATV-type cabling or optical fiber, that can link together a "campus" network of several buildings. The broadband operates as a separate LAN, but there is usually a capability to have several channels for communication. Schools and businesses find such cabling very economical; if the system connects several campuses with wide area network (WAN) links, it is also an alternative to expensive telephone company leases. The WAN links themselves can be dedicated cables or microwave links.

Something that affects many of the information systems we use is client-server technology. This technology uses software processes that run on the server to provide rapid central access to files. Workstations load client software that manages interaction with the user, and, in some cases, data analysis tasks. The value of the technology lies in the distribution of workload between the client and server so that more sophisticated tasks can be performed without overburdening the server with routine user support tasks.

Another prevalent communication problem that some libraries will face, and which involves larger computing systems, is the need to provide terminal access through the LAN. Since the LAN can be attached through a bridge or router to a larger computer, it may be necessary to allow users to access the mainframe by using a suitable terminal protocol. Typically such access involves IBM 3270 (SNA) or DEC VT100 terminal protocols. Although terminal protocols are available entirely as software emulations, a few require hardware as well. Using terminal protocols for large computers in a LAN environment provides tremendous flexibility but carries additional overhead, particularly in extra software.

Remote mini-computer and mainframe terminal access protocols may overload the LAN, the intermediate system (such as a broadband LAN), or the host computer's communication processor. The primary reason for overload is that such communication tends to involve fairly hefty data transmissions, since users do interactive editing and file transfer. The computing is done on the host system rather than the workstation—every keystroke must be transmitted. This is rather unlike typical LAN operations, where site-licensed software is actually run on the local workstation and thus does not cause a direct load on the communication system during task execution. In order to prevent any part of the system from bogging down, invest in the highest speed communication system possible, such as optical fiber. Use can also be limited to essential users.

CONCLUSION

The options for creative communication solutions are very open ended. High-speed data communications are increasingly necessary to support access with graphics-based systems, both for online catalogs and Internet access. Libraries of all types are likely to find products to fit their unique needs in binding their internal operations and users into a productive network environment.

ADDITIONAL RESOURCES

Derfler, Frank J. "The Perfect Network." *PC Magazine* 14(July 1995):224–245.

———. *PC Magazine Guide to Connectivity.* Emeryville, Calif.: Ziff-Davis Press, 1995.

Gaskin, James F. *Novell's Guide to Integrating UNIX and NetWare Networks.* San Jose, Calif.: Novell Press, 1993.

Giorgis, Tadesse W. "29 Switching Hubs Save the Bandwidth." *Byte* 20(July 1995):162–173.

Hurwicz, Michael. "How to Integrate UNIX Servers and NetWare LANs." *Datamation* 40(December 1, 1994):57–59.

Love, J. C. "It's a Management Issue." *PC Magazine* 13(May 31, 1994): 274–276.

Simonds, Fred. *McGraw-Hill LAN Communications Handbook.* New York: McGraw-Hill, 1994.

11 LANS IN LABS

The reasons for operating a microcomputer lab in the library vary greatly, but the concerns about operation of most labs are very similar. Two areas probably account for the most concern: a physical layout that will accommodate the instructional format, and the software environment. Many other issues, such as staffing, access by those with disabilities, and circulation of software, present problems that may already be addressed by library policy.

SETTING UP A LAB

Clear objectives are important when setting up a lab. In some libraries, the lab will be simply a room with lecture seating and a podium computer with a flat-panel projection system. In other libraries, particularly those whose patrons are mostly students, the lab may be equipped with computers that students can use for class exercises and writing papers. Where resources permit, many libraries prefer to have a facility that accommodates both classroom and individual access. Yet another ingredient is that a lab can provide access to the Internet and an increasing number of CD-ROMs, multimedia resources, and remote databases. The choice of configuration will be determined by whether the library requires a staff training facility, a public service facility, or both. The choice of objectives is likely to become more complicated as more resources, such as reading materials, become available in machine-readable format.

LOCATION
Ideally the lab should be adjacent to the LAN manager's office. In many situations the LAN manager also manages the lab. To minimize traffic, public access labs are most often located near the library's main entrance. Such a location not only enhances access but also provides a public relations boost by directing attention to a major investment in technology.

LAYOUT
Configuration of the lab has a number of possibilities that depend on the lab's objectives, particularly whether classroom teaching will be included. In labs arranged for hands-on teaching there are several possible room arrangements. In many labs, computers are arranged around the periphery of the room. This is often done in labs with LANs to facilitate wiring. From an instructional viewpoint this may be less effective because students must

crane around to follow the instructor or to see instructions noted on the blackboard. Something close to a traditional classroom arrangement can be effected with a star wiring topology, although wiring may require butting one end of each row of desks against a wall so that LAN cable and electrical wiring do not have to cross an open space. Flatwire under carpet tile removes this problem by allowing both signal and power cabling to be run unobtrusively to any location in the lab.

In labs where free-flow public access and teaching must occur at the same time, it is normal to have the space divided, most often with glass panels. The glass panels allow staff to supervise both areas when the whole room is used for lab.

PROJECTION

In a lecture-oriented space, one of the primary issues is whether projection systems will present a large enough image and whether the projection equipment will block audience view. Flat-panel liquid crystal display (LCD) systems from vendors like Kodak and Sharp offer the least expensive and possibly most flexible systems. (Be prepared to pay a substantial amount for projection systems, though, because the overhead projector used with a good color LCD must produce at least 5500 lumens.) It is often necessary to place such systems on a low stand and angle the projection screen so that the equipment does not block audience view. Ceiling-mounted projectors offer the best option for keeping the equipment out of the way, but they must be permanently installed because of the difficulty of getting good focus. Older ceiling-mount systems, based on television technology, required low light levels in the room and tended to lose focus in the corner of the screen. New projection systems, with single lens projection, use LCD technology. The newer systems are also small enough to be suitable for portable use. Large television monitors offer another choice with a myriad of options. A large rear-projection system can be easy to see and well focused. Smaller monitors can be used, but it is important to have several of them so that the audience does not strain to see the fine print.

Podiums for LAN-based training systems need careful design because they must hold a great deal. Usually the workstation monitor must be situated so that the instructor can see it from both a seated and a standing position. The keyboard needs to be on a firm surface that is acoustically dead so that key clicks do not distract the audience. Space for a track ball or mouse is needed. Secure storage space in or near the podium is required for manuals and supplies.

WORKSPACE

Setup of individual lab workspaces demands careful planning. Basic workspace features include

- wiring located such that chairs and feet will not injure it
- keyboard placed at comfortable typing level
- space to spread out exercise sheets, reference manuals, and other books
- ready access to power switches
- convenient access to disk drive bays
- clear view of the podium and projection system
- clear aisles to the central printer
- seating for wheelchairs
- a table or cubbyholes near the door for users to stow drinks, backpacks, or other encumbrances

SOFTWARE ENVIRONMENT

Software environment may not seem like an issue if you think that patrons are lucky to have anything at all. If you are providing the services of a LAN, it is likely that many users will be confronted with mystifying aspects of the computing resources. Lab managers generally prefer to confine users to a menu-driven interface—with ready access to tutorials, applications, and communications—that will support novice users. A sub-menu, DOS shell, or other option that a novice will not access by accident can be made available for advanced users who can be trusted with more command of their environment. Another benefit of a menu system is that it invisibly interposes programs to monitor copyright-compliant and virus-free access to software.

Printing needs to be planned to provide a consistent output procedure and to minimize workload for lab staff. An initial intuitive approach is often to connect one dot-matrix printer to two computers and provide an A-B switch for printing. This scheme is unsatisfactory from two standpoints: it requires an unnecessary number of printers, and consequently more staff time, and it places users in an environment they are unlikely to experience in non-academic organizations. A better approach is to set up a print server, which may be a computer dedicated to printer support or it may be an interface that allows the printer to be plugged into the hub. A print server provides the additional value of allowing the lab staff to monitor jobs and to "kill" any that are exceptionally long or are requested killed by the user. A typical situation where this feature is useful is when a student prints a UU-encoded file or a raw postscript file using the word processor, only to see "garbage" being printed.

POLICY PLANNING

Management of a LAN in a lab usually requires more policy planning. Questions that must be asked include

- Will access be allowed for anyone who walks in or will identification be required?
- How will printing be regulated to allow sufficient volume to meet student needs yet not require "printer police"?
- Who will be responsible for startup and shutdown of the lab and the lab LAN?
- How much staff time will be needed, with what mix of skills, to cover the hours of access?
- What scope of assistance will be provided for users and when will it be offered?
- How will conflicts between teaching and public access schedules be resolved?
- How much computer storage space will be made available to each user? Will the user be notified that such space is subject to erasure?
- Will e-mail be available—so users can notify the LAN manager of problems and possibly communicate with each other and the Internet?
- Will students be able to submit homework to instructors via the LAN?

Among the many creative solutions developed for LANs that operate labs, the most successful have provided maximum service with minimum restriction. Happily, a LAN environment guards against software copyright violations and provides most users with ready access to a wide variety of resources.

ADDITIONAL RESOURCES

Hsieh, Cynthia C. "Public-Access Microcomputer Laboratories in Libraries: A Small Academic Library Experience." *Library Software Review* 10(July/August 1991):272–273.
Stanley, Ron. "Local Area Networks and Classroom Anarchy." *Community College Journal 63*(October/November 1992):32–37.
Stigleman Sue E., and Cathryn White. "A Microcomputer Teaching Lab for Information Management Education." *Medical Reference Services Quarterly* 11(spring 1992):67–73.
Wells, David B. "A Dual-Purpose Microcomputer Center: Public Access Facility and Staff Training Lab." *OCLC Micro* 7(February 1991):13–15.

AFTERWORD

Whatever role we envision for local area networks, it is important to keep sight of the purposes libraries have in the world. We can see that there are vital and useful tasks for communications in every aspect of library activities. It is possible to have bookmobiles operate automated checkout systems over cellular telephones using LAN interfaces. It is possible to scan rare books for inter-library loan of the graphic image. Many problems must be solved as national electronic networks grow roots at the local level. A lot of experimentation is still necessary to make many forms of publication available electronically. Librarians have a role to play in an electronic environment where they serve as gatekeepers to various systems. In this role as gatekeeper, they have much work to do to keep users aware of the expanding array of information sources and to make wise choices about whether to locate resources locally or in a cooperative remote environment. As every institution moves the administration of its daily business into electronically networked, transaction processing systems and databases, it will take the vigilance, motivation, and entrepreneurial talents of every librarian to use electronic systems wisely.

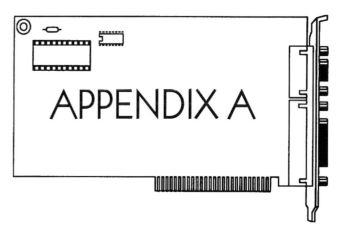

APPENDIX A

LIBRARY NEEDS ANALYSIS FORM

1. What library functions are needed from software operating on the LAN?

    _____ circulation   _____ online catalog
    _____ acquisitions and billing   _____ cataloging
    _____ serials check-in   _____ publicity
    _____ mailing notices and form letters

2. What administrative tasks are needed from software operating on the LAN?

    _____ budgeting   _____ equipment inventory
    _____ appointment scheduling   _____ word processing

3. What problems are routinely encountered that the LAN is intended to remedy?

    _____ slow processing speed in _____
    _____ poor coordination between staff members
    _____ inaccurate record keeping in _____
    _____ lack of ordering/delivery of service to users
    _____ lack of user access to library databases and/or CD-ROMs

4. How many paper book volumes are there in the collection? _____

5. How many circulation transactions are there per week? _____

6. Are workstations already installed in library work areas? ____ yes   __ no

7. How many existing workstations will be attached to the LAN? _____

8. How many workstations will be added to the LAN in the first year? _____

9. What characteristics of the parent organization impact the plan to implement a
    LAN within the library? _____

10. Is there a mainframe or minicomputer available? _____ yes ___ no

    If so, what is the make and model? _____
    What is the operating system? _____
    Is there capacity available for a library application? _____ yes _____ no
    What terminal protocol is used? _____
    What electronic mail system is available? _____

11. Are there LANs in other departments within the organization? ____ yes ___ no

    If so, what LAN operating system is used? _____

12. Is there a backbone network connecting the departmental LANs?

    _____ yes _____ no

    If so, is there a centralized facility for backing up attached LANs?
    _____ yes _____ no

13. Is there assistance available from an internal MIS or computer maintenance department? ___ yes ___ no

14. Does the organization purchase computer hardware and/or software from a central source? _____ yes _____ no

15. Are there existing site licenses?
    For software?   _____ yes _____ no
    For operating system(s)?   _____ yes _____ no

16. Is there a LAN consultant on retainer for the parent organization?

    _____ yes _____ no

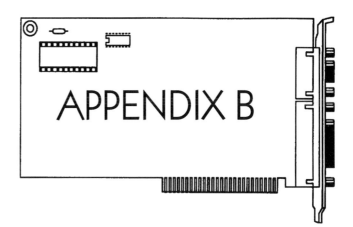

APPENDIX B

USER NEEDS PROFILE

1. What workstation is being used? brand _____

    model _____

2. Does the workstation have a hard disk? yes/no   capacity? _____

3. Which operating system is used? _____ version? _____

4. Which application software is used routinely?

    type: _____   name _____
    type: _____   name _____
    type: _____   name _____
    type: _____   name _____
    type: _____   name _____

5. Who installed the software?

    _____ the vendor
    _____ the Management Information Systems (MIS) department
    _____ I did it myself

6. What printer or output devices are most desirable for your work?

    _____
    _____

7. Please rank your priority for services (1 is highest, 5 is lowest):

    _____electronic mail (in-house)
    _____electronic mail (external)
    _____library catalog
    _____CD-ROM databases
    _____access to external databases

8. Do you work after normal office hours? _____

9. Do you work on Saturday? _____ Sunday? _____

10. What software would you like to have?

    type: _____ name _____

    type: _____ name _____

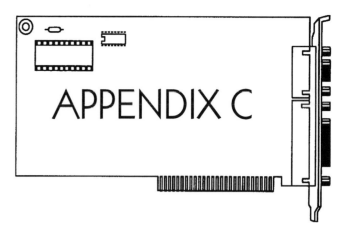

APPENDIX C

LAN OPERATING SYSTEM ENVIRONMENTAL PROFILE

1. What operating systems are currently being used for LANs within the parent organization? _____

2. What operating systems are being used on minicomputers and mainframes in the parent organization? _____

3. Is there a backbone network currently being used between departments of the organization? _____ Will there be in the future ?

4. What operating system is specified for a current or future backbone network?

   _____

5. What workstation environment does the library system of your choice require?

   _____

6. With what network operating system(s) is your library system of choice compatible?

   _____

7. How many workstations are required in the LAN when it is fully configured?

   _____

8. Are there specialized workstations, with unusual operating systems, that must be supported by the LAN?

   _____

9. What type of server will the LAN operate on?

   _____

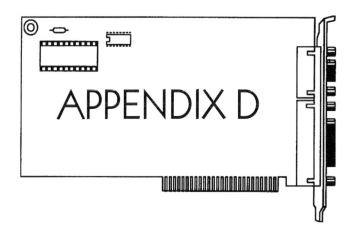

APPENDIX D

SYSTEM RELIABILITY: CHECKING HARDWARE AND SOFTWARE FEATURES

RAID (REDUNDANT ARRAY OF INEXPENSIVE DISKS)

Level	Description
Ø	Data striping, no redundancy
1	Data mirroring, full redundancy
2	Level
3	Data striping at the byte level, single parity drive
4	Data striping in blocks, single parity drive
5	Data striping in blocks, parity rotated across all drives, parity and data on separate drives

RAID is not a magic solution—you must still back up data in order to guard against a catastrophe such as fire or a multiple disk failure. It is wise to have drives from two or more manufacturers. If the disks all come from the same manufacturer and the same production batch, they might all fail together. Purchase and have a spare drive on hand.

RAID comes in two varieties: hardware implementations, where you buy the disks and the software, and *software* implementations, where you can supply disk drives you already own. The hardware packages often have extra features, such as their own power supply, extra controller cards that add to reliability, and an expansible chassis. Look for RAID systems that are hot-swappable, a feature that allows the drive to be replaced without taking the system off line. Also look for battery backup, so the system doesn't lose data during power outages. When you look at magazine reviews, look for MTBF (Mean Time Between Failures) as a guide to reliability. Most good systems are going to be based on some form of the SCSI (small computer systems interface) bus.

SYSTEM FAULT TOLERANCE

Operating systems may provide features that insure some degree of reliability in operation. These features provide capabilities that may require implementation of additional hardware.

Memory. Fault tolerance may be simply in the type of memory chips installed in the server. ECC (error checking and correcting) memory provides insurance against memory failure.

Mirroring. Hardware mirroring is a feature that means some component or all components are provided redundantly. Disk mirroring allows writing to two disks simultaneously from a single disk controller card. Disk duplexing allows writing to two disks simultaneously from two separate disk controller cards. Server mirroring, where there are two servers with matching configurations, is also possible.

Hot fix. Within disk drive systems, the operating system should provide hot fix capability. With this feature, the operating system checks to see that the data it just wrote to a disk can be read. If the data cannot be read, the system notes the bad location in a table and writes the data to a safe location on the disk.

Novell System Fault Tolerance (SFT) levels are as follows:

SFT Level I	read-after-write verification
	hot fix
	directory and FAT duplication
	disk repair utility, VREPAIR
SFT Level II	disk mirroring
	channel mirroring
SFT Level III	server mirroring

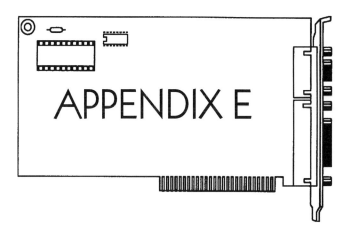

APPENDIX E

DISK SPACE ESTIMATION FORM

LAN name				
Item	Quantity	X	Mb	Total Mb
Operating system		X		
Application - word processor		X		
Application - library system		X		
Application - CD-ROM		X		
Application -		X		
Application -		X		
Application -		X		
Network utility software		X		
Shared files		X		
Print spooling		X		
Network management		X		
Staff users		X		
Guest users*		X		
Other -		X		
Other -		X		
Approximate total space required				

*Guest users include online public access catalog (OPAC) users and CD-ROM users. The space is used for work files that the OPAC or CD-ROM software requires.

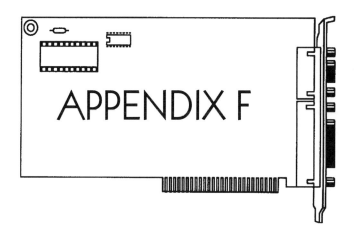

APPENDIX F

NETWORK BACKUP PROCEDURE

1. Check to be sure the network printer is online and has paper.
2. Boot and log in as Supervisor from the machine that has the tape or disk drive that you will backup to.
3. Disable LOGIN so that users cannot log in and keep files open. (Open files are not usually backed up.)
4. Send a courteous broadcast message to all users to log out.
5. Check to be sure no other users are currently on the LAN.
6. Use a network utility or operating system command to clean up directory space on the LAN hard disk(s) ("Purge all salvageable files" in Novell).
7. Use an operating system utility (i.e., LARCHIVE in Novell) to archive the "bindery" files to a floppy disk.
8. Insert a tape or disk in the backup drive.
9. Start the backup software. *(Choose an option to back up file-by-file rather than an option to back up into one big backup file)*
10. When the backup is finished, use TREE, VTREE, or a similar utility to print a hierarchical list of directory names for each hard disk volume in the LAN.
11. Place the directory list printout in the backup folder and return the backup tape and folder to their normal shelf location.
12. Enable LOGIN and return the LAN to normal operation.

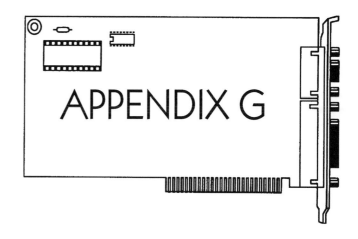

APPENDIX G

TOPOLOGIES

Star Topology

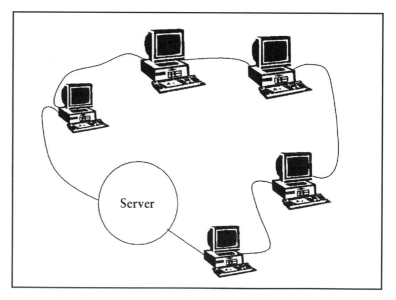

Ring Topology

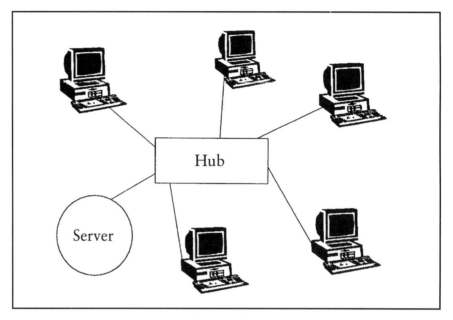

Hub Topology

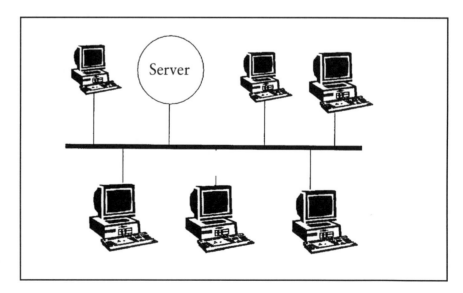

Backbone (Bus)Topology

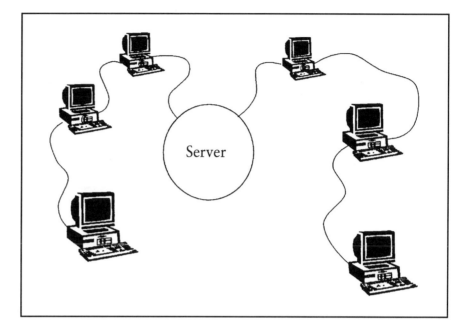

Point-to-Point (Bus) Topology

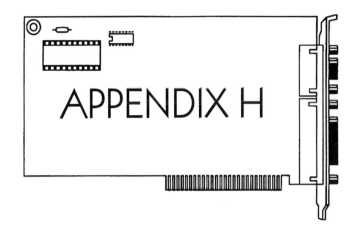

APPENDIX H

WIRING SURVEY

1. What spaces are available for running wiring?
    a. ceilings _____
    b. floors _____
    c. walls _____
    d. utility conduits between floors _____
    e. stairwells _____

2. Are there obstacles that will consume extra cable length (e.g., partitions that rise above a suspended ceiling, building structural components in unusual places, electric motors that may cause interference, air conditioning ducts) in any of these locations?

    _____
    _____
    _____
    _____
    _____

3. Measure distances: on a scale drawing, locate the site for each workstation and estimate the total distance for bus and star topologies. Don't forget to include the distance for wiring up/down walls and around obstacles. Servers for either topology should be located in roughly the geographic center of the LAN. Workstations must be located near electrical outlets.
    a. Total wiring length for bus _____
    b. Total wiring length for star _____

4. Is there any location where cable cannot be run or where it would be extremely inconvenient to run a wire?

    _____
    _____
    _____

5. How much flexibility is required for moving workstations to either rearrange offices or to accommodate facility maintenance?

_____

_____

_____

6. Are there locations such as circulation where cabling will have to be routed through furniture?

_____

_____

_____

7. Specify on the scale drawing where printers will be located. Each printer must either be attached to the server or have a network interface that allows it to be attached as a workstation. Printers must be located in secure areas.

_____

_____

8. Where will wiring hubs be located? Normally wiring hubs are located near the server to facilitate trouble shooting.

_____

9. Are there locations where holes will have to be bored in concrete, masonry, brick or other materials requiring special drills and possibly treatment to preserve the decor?

_____

_____

_____

NEW CONSTRUCTION

1. Can conduits for network wiring be included in the construction?

   _____

2. Can wiring be installed in the conduits, ready for terminations?

   _____

3. Are server areas specified with built-in counters and cabinets, power outlets, and access to the wiring conduits?

   _____

4. Will all blueprint modifications be cleared with the library prior to actual construction so that changes that affect total wiring length are known?

   _____

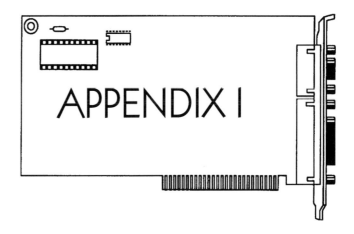

APPENDIX I

SELECTING LIBRARY SYSTEMS

- Consider size and number of patrons in choosing the type of system. If there is more than one library or if the library has a large number of users and workstations, a UNIX system may be appropriate.
- Expect to have a sophisticated interface that allows all of the library electronic systems, including the catalog, CD-ROMs, and Internet access on each terminal.
- User terminals should be personal computers, not dumb terminals.
- The system should facilitate communication with patrons, whether they are able to access the system from a branch location, a work location, or from home. This means having messages that can be seen by the user when they look up patron status or even a complete email subsystem.
- Expect to have good on-screen icons or menus and helps that make additional guides and handouts unnecessary.
- The interface should accommodate every type of user. That means giving the user the choice between browsing and doing a full Boolean search with truncation and field qualifications. It means having a children's interface if that is called for. It means having large print screens for those with limited vision. It means having special keyboard drivers for those with limited dexterity.
- Staff should have system access that has as good an interface as the patrons, with simple access to codes and processes without cumbersome command sequences.
- Where possible, search expansion in the catalog should be possible through hypertext links that allow information from a current record to be used as the input for further search.
- System reliability should be insured, particularly through some of the same features found in the system reliability appendix.
- Software parameters such as library branches, user categories, user interface options, and staff security options should be configurable locally.

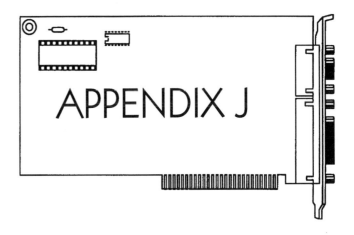

APPENDIX J

SAMPLE USER ACCOUNT INFORMATION FORM

NETWORK ACCOUNT INFORMATION

Library LAN

USER NAME: Jane Kleiner   INITIALIZED: July 19, 1996

INITIAL PASSWORD: DSNGRW   (You MUST change this password the first time you log in.)

ACCOUNT STATUS: active, current

NETWORK GROUPS BELONGED TO: everyone, lanassist, reference

WORDPERFECT OFFICE GROUPS BELONGED TO: everyone, reference, depthead

---

To use the network follow these steps;

1. Turn on your workstation.
2. At the DOS prompt type NET;
    after several moments you will get a new F:\LOGIN> prompt.
3. Enter LOGIN, a space, and your User Name.

Data to be shared between users should be saved into the directory named \SHARED. Confidential data should be saved to your \HOME\ <USERNAME> directory. Confidential data to be shared between staff members should be stored in the \STAFF directory. (To see how to access different directories, use the MAP command at a network prompt.)

Passwords are changed every 40 days. Theses changes are automatically initated by the operating system. Passwords must be between 6 and 15 characters in length and must not duplicate recently used passwords. Alter your password at once if another person gains knowledge of it.

Use virus-scanning software to check all diskettes used on other computers.

Please check your mail at least weekly.

Report problems that occur with the LAN to Ann Smythe, the LAN Manager, at extension 5634.

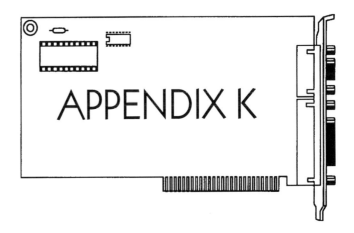

SAMPLE JOB DESCRIPTION

LOCAL AREA NETWORK MANAGER

FUNCTION OF JOB

This is a professional position that requires specialized technical knowledge to develop and maintain a PC-based local area network (LAN). The LAN manager will have primary responsibility for LAN strategic planning and operations in consultation with his/her supervisor as needed. The employee works with other library employees and may supervise clerical personnel in the course of completing projects.

Examples of Work (These examples are intended only as illustrations of the various types of work performed in positions allocated to this class.)

> evaluate, select, acquire, and install network resources
> troubleshoot network users' computer problems
> administer security controls for user access, software, data, and communication channels
> develop a budget for current and projected network needs
> establish procedures for systems modifications and problem control
> educate users about network services
> participate in professional activities and programs for developing network management skills
> develop and implement policies and procedures for all the above items

REQUIRED QUALIFICATIONS

Bachelor's degree or equivalent combination of experience, education, and training for supporting large numbers of computer users, with responsibility for hardware, software, application support, and user training. Also requires

- working knowledge of Novell NetWare or similar networking operating systems

- knowledge of MS-DOS operating systems and micro-computer hardware
- working knowledge of data communications concepts
- knowledge of local area network wiring and trouble-shooting

RECOMMENDED QUALIFICATIONS

- ability to program in one higher level language, preferrably Pascal or C Language
- one to three years management experience with responsibility for budget and staff
- excellent oral and written communication skills
- proficiency with an advanced word processor such as Microsoft Word or WordPerfect
- proficiency with an advanced spreadsheet such as Lotus 1-2-3 or Quattro
- experience with data backup systems
- knowledge of a variety of printers including Postscript laser printers

DUTIES

The LAN manager is responsible for installing, maintaining, and updating the network and the network operating system. This includes

- maintaining a knowledge of the "state of the art" in network technology
- keeping track of documentation for network hardware and software
- maintaining inventory accountability for network hardware
- routinely backing up data and programs located on the network server
- troubleshooting hardware and software problems
- purchasing new hardware and software
- tracking and reporting network use statistics
- attending off-site meetings relating to LAN operations
- assisting in development of policies for users

The LAN manager is also responsible for configuring the network software to support users in the most user-friendly manner possible. This includes establishing print queues and print formats, establishing local menus, establishing security and confidentiality procedures for access and data storage, operating the system during hours convenient to users.

COMMENTS

This position description was formulated to provide a baseline to guide managers in creating LAN manager positions in a variety of environments, including academic, government, and business libraries. The description avoids specifying the scope of the LAN supported, the number of users supported, additional duties, and familiarity with specific applications software or types of workstations.

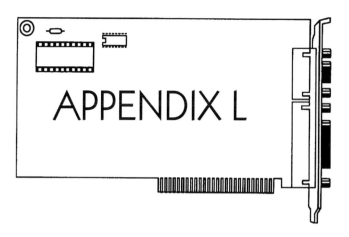

APPENDIX L

CHECKLIST FOR MAJOR UPGRADES

____ 1. Back up the files on all LAN hard-disk volumes. Be sure to include bindery information (security and file ownership information).

____ 2. Print the directory structure of the LAN hard disks so that you can rebuild it if necessary. Print a list of all current users.

____ 3. Print out the configuration files for print spoolers and mail systems that are likely to be critical to LAN operations.

____ 4. Decrement the counters of any applications with a counter that limits the number of simultaneous users.

____ 5. Check to make sure you know the location of the original copy of the LAN operating system that you used for installation. Locate phone numbers for software and hardware vendors and be sure you have current Internet or Compuserve access so you can download driver updates and diagnostic programs as needed.

____ 6. Proceed to upgrade hardware, operating system, or applications software as required. If you are upgrading a hard disk or the entire server including hard disk, try to arrange for the old hard disk or server to be kept on the shelf for a week while you get the system through a shakedown cruise.

____ 7. Reload the data files and bindery files. Be sure to use facilities in your backup program to restore files selectively. If the operating system was upgraded you DO NOT want to reload the operating system or any of its utilities.

____ 8. Check the directory structure to insure that all directories are reloaded and in place.

____ 9. Revise batch files and menus to accommodate changes resulting from the upgrade.

____ 10. Log in on a user account and check to see that all of the applications software works, that users can find their data files, and that the configurations for printers and screen drivers are set properly.

____ 11. Post a notice on the user bulletin board or help screens detailing changes in the system.

____ 12. Document configuration changes in your paper records concerning the LAN. Mail in warranty cards for upgraded items.

____ 13. Update user manuals, local policies, and local user aids.

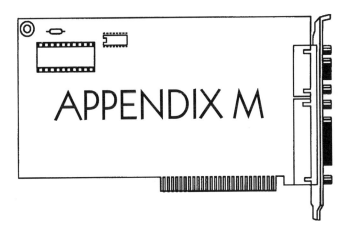

APPENDIX M

EQUIPMENT MAINTENANCE RECORD		
ITEM & MODEL NO.:		
WARRANTY PERIOD:		
SERIAL NO.: INVENTORY NO.:		
PO#	PO DATE / /	RECEIVED / /
VENDOR NAME:		
PHONE NO.:		
ADDRESS:		
CONFIGURATION NOTES		
MAINTENANCE VENDOR NAME:		
PHONE NO.:		
ADDRESS:		

PROBLEM	DATE CALLED IN	SPOKE TO
NOTES		
NOTES		
NOTES		
MISCELLANEOUS		

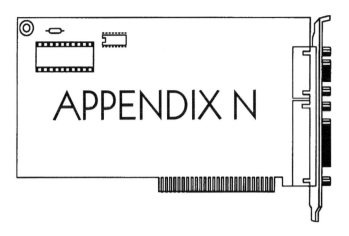

APPENDIX N

SAMPLE VIRUS POLICY STATEMENT

POLICY STATEMENT REGARDING COMPUTER VIRUSES

Computer viruses can infect critical computer systems at any time. We have been lucky in finding that our security perimeter was sufficiently tight to withstand infection thus far, but we may not be so fortunate in the future. This policy statement is intended to provide guidance that will provide even better protection in the future.

Every one of us should be aware that any diskette or any files that are transmitted electronically or downloaded are possible sources of infection. Please treat all disks and downloads, even if they are provided by seemingly irreproachable sources or not, with caution.

DECONTAMINATION
1. Disks brought into the library and files transmitted electronically should be scanned by virus detecting software before being used in any way.
2. All disks are subject to challenge. If a disk is not submitted for screening, the owner will not be permitted to use it on workstations in the library. Use of unscanned disks may be a basis for disciplinary action.

LAB PROCEDURES
1. Users will follow decontamination procedures for all disks brought into the lab. If lab personnel are not available, users should contact the nearest staff person for assistance.
2. Users are not permitted to use administrative computers in other parts of the library to complete lab exercises.
3. *All* software packages installed on all computers, including demonstration programs, are subject to this policy.

DISCOVERY PROTOCOL

1. Infected disks will be reported to the LAN manager. Since removal of a virus may require relatively drastic measures such as reformatting hard disks, only the LAN manager or personnel designated by the LAN manager will implement cleanup procedures.
2. The LAN manager or the manager's assistant should notify the MicroComputer Support Office of any viruses discovered, noting the date, type of virus, and type of disk that was infected.

PREVENTION

1. Floppy disks or electronically transmitted files must be scanned before use.
2. In labs, be sure that the system is cold booted when a workstation is turned over for use by someone else. A warm boot could very easily leave a virus stored untouched in memory.
3. When an outside microcomputer system such as another server is accessed, the workstation should be cold booted immediately after the user logs out of the remote system. This includes such services as the library server where CD-ROM services are available.
4. Users should be aware that files attached to e-mail messages, specifically those files that are programs (software), may be infected with viruses.
5. Please insure that security precautions for the LAN are followed. Passwords should not be shared. Compromised passwords should be changed or reported to the LAN manager.
6. Establishing a virus-free environment for home computer systems will help prevent problems. Make other users of home systems aware of the potential problems. Use virus-scanning software. Carefully scan all software obtained from bulletin boards and swap meets.
7. Virus software must be kept current to preclude new viruses from becoming established.

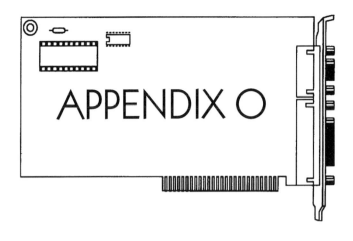

GLOSSARY

Applications software: Microcomputer software that allows information to be used or manipulated in some way. General purpose applications include word processing, spreadsheet, and information retrieval software. Special purpose applications include accounting, library operations, and games.

ASCII: American Standard Code for Information Interchange (ASCII) is the most generic data coding format for representing data and programs in binary format. Microcomputer users often use ASCII as a synonym for DOS format when they are talking about data files. What is usually understood is that data in ASCII format have no special escape codes or other unusual features that a word processor or database program would enter into a file.

Background: Some combinations of operating system and hardware allow multiprocessing (i.e., tasks can be performed simultaneously). A program that runs in the background is not seen by the user and results are usually reported when the task is complete.

Batch Files: Operating system files that contain operating system commands are called batch files and usually have the suffix .BAT in microcomputers. In a LAN environment, batch files may include commands from the workstation operating system or from the LAN operating system.

Bindery files: Coded information denoting which user account has security access to which directories and files is kept in the bindery. Decisions about security are usually made over a long period of time and the bindery reflects the most recent decisions.

Booting: Computers can be started two ways. One way is to "cold boot" the system by turning the power switch on. The other way is to restart the system by pressing a reset switch—a "warm boot."

Bridge: A bridge usually connects two different computer systems in a manner that is invisible or barely visible to the user. The command interface does not change over a bridge, even though the user may have to cross boundaries where new passwords are required. It is possible for the cabling, and in some cases even the signal technology, to differ on either side of a bridge, provided that the operating system remains the same.

Buffer: Space in memory can be set aside so that data coming or going to the LAN, to the printer, or being sorted can use the space temporarily.

Bus: Any electrical connection between parts of a system. Bus is used to describe both the traces on a computer's mother board that connect the accessory cards and any relatively linear type of LAN wiring between computers.

Compatibility: For software, compatibility means that the program is written to operate with a certain type of computer. Drivers provided with the software may make the software capable of operating with specific monitors, printers, and other peripheral devices. For hardware, compatibility usually means that, with proper mechanical and electrical connections, two devices can exchange signals. Usually compatibility involves standards, such as those specified by professional associations, industry or consumer groups, or by de facto acceptance.

Configuration: Configuration generally encompasses all of the hardware and software variables that can be customized for the user's convenience or in support of an objective. Configuration is important because computer programs need to know how much memory they can work with, whether the screen display is monochrome or color, what kind of printer to expect, and where to find DOS files and other needed programs.

Desktop software: Two types of program make up the category of desktop software. One type is the graphical user interface (GUI) that uses icons to represent files and software. Another type of desktop is a menu-driven system, presented as text, that has utilities such as a calendar, calculator, and rolodex. Both systems have the objective of helping the user find tools and files easily and use the desktop environment as a homebase within the computer system.

DOS (disk operating system): Personal computers most often use a Microsoft operating system that provides basic access and operation of the computer. The most recent version of DOS is version 6; version 7 is on the way. Alternative operating systems with virtually identical functions are available; DR DOS is one example.

Downing the server: A command given at the keyboard of the server can shut down the LAN server. When a server is shut down in this way, files and user logins are terminated in a safe manner.

Driver: Auxiliary programs that provide a special feature or allow connection of the computer to a specialized device are called drivers. Drivers may be installed so that you can use a mouse, a printer, a color monitor, a LAN interface card, or a CD-ROM. Drivers may be loaded into workstation memory during boot-up or by an applications program such as a word processor.

Foreground: Some combinations of operating system and hardware allow multiprocessing (i.e., tasks can be performed simultaneously). A program executing in the foreground may interact with the user and usually shows screen displays and intermediate results to the user.

Gateway: A connection between two computer systems that have significantly different user interfaces is called a gateway. Abrupt changes in protocol usually involve two drastically different systems, such as a LAN and a mainframe computer, or two different operating systems, such as DOS and UNIX.

GUI: A graphical user interface (GUI) places the user in an environment where the user has greater intuitive control of the computer than in a command-driven environment or a menu system. In a GUI environment some commands and all applications programs are displayed to the user as graphic objects or "icons" (for instance, a picture of a book to represent a library software package).

Hub: Hubs connect multiple computers both together and to any external network. Most twisted pair wired LANs connect to some kind of hub. In a LAN, the server connects to the hub—that's how it connects to the other computers.

Hypertext: Many software packages provide links between the current screen display and other information stored on the local computer or another computer system. The link is made visible by text that is a different color, bold, or bracketed by special characters.

Internet: Beginning with government initiatives in the 1960s, industrial, educational, and governmental organizations began to link their computers so that users could transport data, send electronic mail, and share collaborative efforts. This network has gradually become more commercialized, but is in an interesting way still "voluntary." With its high level of commercial, scientific, and educational use it has become an integral part of many organizations.

Interoperability: An ideal environment for users would be provided by systems that provide "transparent" access to users connected through gateways and bridges. Applications that "interoperate" allow users to convey data, while operating within the application, between disparate computer systems.

LAN: A local area network (LAN) is a group of microcomputers that are connected via communication media and that utilize common software to exchange data and perform such tasks as printing. Scope of a LAN is usually within one building or department.

MAN: A metropolitan area network (MAN) is a group of interconnected local area networks (LANS) that spans an industrial or educational complex; essentially a "campus" network. A MAN typically involves a backbone network utilizing broadband technology and is increasingly likely to involve fiber optic cabling.

Menu: A menu program lists items on the computer screen for the user to choose from. Menu systems are particularly helpful to novice users and require less sophisticated software and hardware than graphical user interfaces (GUIs).

Multitasking: An operating system is capable of multitasking if it can provide several users with service at what is apparently the same time. If the system is truly capable of multiprocessing, users can access part of the memory and computing logic of the computer simultaneously. If the system does not multiprocess, it may still be fast enough to allow multitasking by providing each user short periods of exclusive use of the memory and logic.

Operating system: Software that makes the computer operational is called an operating system. Some part of the operating system software is required to be in memory at all times; other portions may have to be readily accessible on disk. The operating system provides reliable access to memory, the computer processor, and peripheral devices for applications software. Normally an operating system is specific to a particular species of hardware.

Platform: The type of computer used for a computing system is called a platform. To a certain extent, specific operating systems, size of application, and computing power are implied by noting the platform to be used.

Plug-compatible: Computer devices are plug-compatible when connections can be made with standard plugs that match mechanically and electronically. Ideally, devices should be plug-compatible as they come off the retailer's shelf.

Protocol: A standard means of communicating data between computers or a standard means of interaction between a program and the user is termed a protocol.

Real time: Computers can be used so that events represented by computer data keep pace with events in the real world. This applies, for example, to library circulation systems that process transactions rapidly enough to yield such information as that a patron has overdue books and is blocked for circulation.

Router: Connecting different networks may require a router, which is similar in many respects to a bridge. Routers tend to examine each packet of information sent along the network to determine if it should be forwarded. Routers are primarily used where cabling and protocols do not change.

Sneaker net: When people move data between computers by writing it to disk at one machine and then carrying the disk to the other machine, they form a sneaker (hand-carried) network.

Spooling: Software can "spool" information intended for the printer by storing it temporarily in a disk file. Thus a word processor or the DOS print command can format several jobs for the printer and stack them up, to await access to the printer. Normally, spooled jobs go to the printer on a first-come-first-served basis. In many situations, such as with the DOS print command or in a LAN, printing priorities may be adjusted to move priority jobs ahead in the queue.

Topology: The scheme by which connections are made between parts of a network is called the topology. Typical topologies include bus (linear), star (centralized), and ring (multiple connections).

User friendly: Ideally every software package should present the user with a menu or list of functions that the program performs. In addition, each software package should have a means of avoiding the menu system and going to a simple interface where commands can be entered. Obviously, the definition of user friendly varies from person to person.

WAN: A wide area network (WAN) is a group of interconnected local area networks (LANS) that span a distance in such a manner that a major connection between parts of the network involves dedicated telecommunication circuits equivalent to long-distance telephone circuits.

World Wide Web: The Internet provides sufficient communication speed that messages can incorporate text, graphics, and sound clips. World Wide Web service is provided by institutions that set up a special server on the

Internet to provide access to multimedia information. Users access the server information with client software such as Netscape, Mosaic, and Lynx. Local Internet access providers also provide Web or "homepage" servers. Information in the Web is formatted with hypertext links that allow rapid navigation between pieces of information, wherever they may be located. Subject search capability is provided by a number of organizations, some of which charge for access to their database.

INDEX

Administration, 5
Air-conditioning, 53
Applications, 43, 44, 63, 66
Backup, 31, 65
Bridge, 29
CD-ROM, 92–93
Computer literacy, 68
Connections, 39, 69, 91-94
Costs, 46
Daily operations, 71
Databases, 4, 6, 48
Disk space management, 24–25, 64
Drivers, 45
E-Mail, 6, 17, 44, 69
Ethernet, 16, 28, 29
Files, 6, 14, 15, 24, 56, 65, 68, 69
Games, 59
Gateways, 29
Hardware, 23, 54, 73
Internet, 27
Labs, 7, 97
LAN Manager, 8, 20, 27, 36, 57, 61, 64,
    66, 67, 74
Library systems, 3, 47, 64
Manuals, 50, 52
Modems, 92
Objectives, 84, 97
Operating system, 12, 54–56
Outlets, 37

Physical security, 33, 73
Planning, 7, 51, 97
Policy, 36
Printer spooling, 19, 28, 33, 52, 67
Printers, 27, 99
Purchasing, 51
Retrieval systems, 48
Retrospective conversion, 48
Security, 32, 66, 69, 78, 85
Server, 11, 23, 24
Set up, 53, 54, 78–79
Sharing, 11, 44, 56, 68
Space, 37, 52, 65, 97, 100
Staff, 62, 85
Start up, 9, 51
Sub-LANs, 19
Supervisor, 67
Supplies, 2, 38–39
Systems analysis, 82
Tool kit, 38, 72
Training 9, 49–50, 58–59, 61–63, 68
Uninterruptible power supply, 31
UNIX, 13
Upgrade, 9
Usage tracking, 20, 66
Users, 3, 58, 63, 69–70
Viruses, 17, 49, 78
Wireless, 40
Wiring, 35, 38, 75
Workstations, 12, 25, 26, 33, 57

COLOPHON

Norman Howden has served as an academic information specialist, founded and managed a marine science information center at LSU, and taught in Schools of Library and Information Science. He currently works as a Librarian at El Centro College and as an Information Specialist at the Business Information Center in the Cox School of Business at Southern Methodist University, both in Dallas. Dr. Howden has conducted funded projects and authored a number of journal articles, books, and thesauruses in Library and Information Science. His areas of special interest include library systems technology, management of technology resources, database production, and indexing of information. Previously he was Chair of the Texas Chapter of the American Society for Information Science and Chair of the Education, Training, and Support Committee, Machine Accessible Reference Section, Reference and Adult Services Division, of the American Library Association. Currently, he serves as the American Library Association representative on the Board of Directors for Documentation Abstracts, Inc. which is responsible for Information Science Abstracts.